I hope this Book
inspires you to
also remember the
human connection
a you young toward
exemplary leadership.

Lisa

Also by Lisa I. Perez

The Younger Self Letters Anthology
ASIN: B095V9X9M3
Publisher: Monarch Crown Publishing (May 25, 2021)
Publication date: May 25, 2021

THE COMPLETE MANAGER MAKEOVER

Transforming the Human in Human Resources®

Lisa I. Perez, SPHR, SHRM-SCP

authorHOUSE®

AuthorHouse™
1663 Liberty Drive
Bloomington, IN 47403
www.authorhouse.com
Phone: 833-262-8899

Published by AuthorHouse 06/30/2021

ISBN: 978-1-6655-2954-9 (sc)
ISBN: 978-1-6655-2959-4 (hc)
ISBN: 978-1-6655-2958-7 (e)

Library of Congress Control Number: 2021912284

Print information available on the last page.

DEDICATION

This book is dedicated to my big brother,
Laval J. Brown Jr., a.k.a. Chipper.
We were supposed to be doing so
much of this journey together,
but I always hear you whispering, GO ACHIEVE!

CONTENTS

FOREWORD

I will never forget the time I first met Lisa Perez. It was in a training program she attended. The reason I remember her is because of her unique D/S personality blend. That particular blend is a little more uncommon. Of course, there is nothing wrong with it –it is just a little more statistically unusual – which perfectly describes Lisa. She is no average or ordinary person. She is a trailblazer doing her best to make a positive difference in the life of everyone she meets.

Perhaps you have heard the positive, exciting, motivational saying, "There is one in every crowd"; well, that would be Lisa! She has the energy of a Cheetah, the tenacity of a Lion, the compassion of Mother Teresa and the heart of a Champion. Try finding that combination in most people!

This new book she has written will open your eyes to see things you have not understood in the past. In a world full of self-help books, who would even attempt to include another one? Only someone who had something new and different and important to communicate...which Lisa does. I am so grateful for all she has to say!

Writing a book is both a labor of toil and yet a labor of love. No one understands what all is included in that process until they have done it. That is why less than 1% of people on the planet will ever do it. The key element is having a message that will make a difference in the life of the reader and then the long and toilsome effort it takes to complete the task. Lisa has done it!

The reader is in for a treat in his or her own personal growth and development journey. The information you are about to read will make that journey more profitable and enjoyable. Thank you, Lisa. For a job well done! I am proud of you!

Robert A. Rohm, Ph.D.
Personality Insights, Inc.
Atlanta, GA

AUTHORS NOTE

10% of the proceeds from The Complete Manager Makeover (The CMM) book sales, products & services are donated to 501c3 organizations for their clean water initiatives. They include TheWaterBearers™ whose mission is to inspire those who have access to clean water to get it to those who do not and Blood:Water whose vision is to end the water and HIV/AIDS crises in Africa.

This link https://thecompletemanagermakeover.com/thecmm/cmm-supplemental-toolkit/ is for The CMM Supplemental Workbook & Toolkit which provides sample forms and additional information that can support your managerial function while providing best practice processes to enhance your role in the respective topic. The Appendix contains additional guides and checklists to help you execute many of the processes suggested in this book. These forms and documents have universal application within any organization. If you find that your company does not have a sufficient human resources compliance and training infrastructure, consider The Complete Manager Makeover Memberships that provide valuable resources and benefits to meet those needs.

This book is designed to provide accurate and authoritative information regarding the subject matter covered. It is sold with the understanding that neither the publisher nor the author is engaged in rendering legal advice. If legal advice or other expert assistance is required the services of a competent licensed or certified professional should be sought. As laws may vary by state and are subject to frequent amendment, this book addresses Federal Employment law regulations and their general application to most private sector employers. The federal laws discussed in this book are subject to frequent revision and interpretation by amendments or judicial revisions that may significantly affect employer and employee rights and obligations. State regulations, Affirmative Action employers and Public Sector Employer regulations and Collective Bargaining Agreements may vary;

therefore, before taking any actions on the information contained in this book individuals should review this material with internal/ external counsel, company HR Representatives or the services of HBL Resources, Inc. a full-service human resource consulting firm, to determine specific applicability. Our founder can be reached at info@thecompletemanagermakeover.com. The interpretations conclusions and recommendations in this book are those of the authors are not necessarily representing those of the publisher.

ACKNOWLEDGEMENTS

There are so many people to thank who have made this book possible, many have had a direct impact and are aware of their contributions, but there are countless others who have had an impact on my career in some way, whose stories intersected with mine whether for a moment or for a season there are so many it would be impossible to name them all, nonetheless...

- to my parents who instilled in me an anything is possible attitude and modeled the entrepreneurial spirit and drive that continues to be my inspiration.
- to my children and siblings who have cheered me on at every step of this entrepreneurial journey, thank you for believing in me and stepping up to help when I needed you.
- to my husband Mark, who has believed in me and cheered me at the sidelines and told me "you got this" when I needed it the most, thank you for your encouragement throughout the years.
- to the countless general managers and colleagues with whom I've worked, thank you for the lessons learned, the support through tough times, the laughter, the grace, the triumph, the camaraderie.
- to the many mentors, coaches, teachers, authors, and trainers that have been part of my journey, thank you for the encouragement, guidance, instruction, and foundational principles you imparted.
- to Michelle San Juan who took the time to help me edit this book, I'm forever grateful for your second set of eyes and the invaluable feedback you provided.
- most of all, to God Almighty who has awakened this purpose in me and supplies all my needs to see this through to completion, I continue to put it all in your hands.

INTRODUCTION

I have always tried to stay on top of statistics and analytics. Even before AI and the technologies of today, I often created my own spreadsheets to track performance analytics in my workplace and organizations. I always believed analytics were important so that you could affect changes based on the findings. I've also believed what is not tracked and measured is not improved and that if you do not inspect what you expect, your expectations will not be met. I read a Work Institutes 2020 Retention Report as I often do, here are a few excerpts particularly related to the lack of development opportunities and manager behavior:

- *The top 3 categories for leaving in 2019 were Career Development (19.6%), Work-Life Balance (12.4%), and Manager Behavior (11.8%)*
- *Interviewees who gave a "poor" rating to their previous employer, supervisor, and job primarily chose manager behavior for their most important reason to leave...*
- *78% of the reasons employees quit could have been prevented by the employer...*
- *Manager behavior is a red flag and getting worse. Organizations must ensure managers are well-trained in relationship skills and conduct or continue to lose the talent war."*

I can't recall the first time I saw statistics like these. What I do recall is that time and time again, year after year, it has remained relatively unchanged. The surveys, for years, have continued to show that employees don't leave jobs or companies they leave BAD managers. I'm an eternal optimist in that I really don't believe in BAD managers, I do however believe in UNTRAINED managers. There are many who argue that the same organizations that have the product and service offerings to improve these statistics are the ones reporting on them, the fact remains these statistics have not been proven to be false. Yet they remain. According to a Society for Human Resource Management (SHRM) 2020 survey, 60% of employees say managers are the reason they left their company. I can only imagine how much worse it will be in future surveys considering what the workforce had to navigate during a global pandemic.

The Complete Manager Makeover, the Transforming the Human in Human Resources® movement, and the founding of National Management Training week establishes a trifecta that endeavors to change these statistics and move the needle by not only providing practical methods, insight and tangible ways for managers to manage, lead, communicate and treat employees, but also to bring both national awareness to the need for better management training and preparedness during a dedicated period of time for organizations to implement these training processes. There is an age-old debate regarding whether great leaders are born or made. It is my opinion that great leaders are born but can also BE MADE. One day these statistics will drastically decrease and no longer show that employees leave bad managers because we have developed better managers, good managers, GREAT managers, and leaders.

Every great leader and manager from as far back as Napoleon Hill and Steven Covey to today's contemporaries like Les Brown and John Maxwell, provide many of these essential concepts and principles. I am no different because there are certain core beliefs and behaviors within me that are responsible for the way I choose to manage, lead, communicate, and motivate people around me. Whether you prefer the word "leader" over "manager" is unimportant. The primary difference between leaders and managers is that leaders have people who follow them while managers have people who work with them, both roles are equally important. Whether you call yourself a manager or a leader is irrelevant because at the core and foundation of both, in my opinion, is to always ensure that, regardless of the conversation, that individual, whether a prospective employee, current employee or a soon to be ex-employee, your responsibility, as a manager and/or leader, is *"to ensure that individual walks out of your office with their dignity intact"*. That is an original Lisa Perez quote! From the very beginning of my HR career as an HR Clerk over 30 years ago, I have believed, led, and managed by that principle and you will see it weaved throughout this book and the curriculum, especially throughout the sections of this book where practical application is provided.

It is because of that core foundational principle, that, to this day, I have great relationships with many of the colleagues that I had to coach, counsel, provide corrective feedback, or even lay off and terminate from employment. Their dignity was always kept intact. I hope this book provides a solid road map, some encouragement, direction, and support on how to be a constructive people manager as you journey towards great leadership. I believe that the first step toward great leadership is knowing how to treat, communicate, motivate, and generally manage and then be able to lead people.

In addition to this book, there is supporting information, additional resources and activities that can help solidify the knowledge. Whether you are a new or seasoned manager, much can be gained by reading this book and completing the activities or using the processes suggested in the workbook supplement that you can obtain The CMM Supplemental Workbook & Toolkit via download at https://thecompletemanagermakeover.com/ thecmm/cmm-supplemental-toolkit/

There are hundreds of books on leadership and management but The Complete Manager Makeover offers a nuts-and-bolts approach to answer questions like "what exactly do I say and do in this situation?" It provides a road map to follow with people management, so whether you are hiring, interviewing, training, or managing performance this book has it all. You'll learn regulatory compliance with practical application including what to do, what to say, and how to modify what you say depending on the person and situation. The free Supplemental Toolkit gives you additional materials and tools to manage your most important career asset, the people.

I hope that you will find the journey through this material enjoyable while providing new, helpful, and valuable ideas and insights regarding the way you manage and lead people. Enjoy the journey.

CHAPTER 1

FUNDAMENTAL PHILOSOPHIES

One of Merriam Webster's definitions of the word philosophy is as follows:

the most basic beliefs, concepts, and attitudes of an individual or group

This chapter highlights some of my fundamental philosophies that I hold dear as they have provided sound guidance and direction throughout my personal and professional experiences, I hope they will constructively guide and direct the beginnings of your transformation.

Fundamental Philosophy #1: Know When to Pivot To Pursue Your Passion

I grew up in Brooklyn, NY. My father was a glazier and owned his own business, this was my first real view of entrepreneurship and I knew at 8 years old that I'd be a business owner one day, but that's another book. My mother was a legal secretary and I wanted to be just like her too. When I was young and had days off from school, I would often get an opportunity to go with her to work. This was way before any Take Your Child To Work Day was an official thing. Mom had always worked in law offices and I recall being able to staple papers, seal envelopes and file papers that sharpened my alphabetizing skills (mom was crafty to ensure learning with that one).

1

I loved everything about administrative work. I would watch my mother on the IBM Selectric Typewriter (google it for fun), zipping away through her dictation, in awe of how quickly her fingers moved and enjoying the unique sound made by the rattling of the font ball, or whatever that element was called. Mom was an excellent legal secretary and I remember she could type 101 words per minute. It was always my goal to beat that record, I came close at 96 once but never did beat her record. Later I would attend Murray Bertram High School for Secretarial Sciences as I recall it (now called Business Careers), and I thrived at all my core courses like stenography, typing and office administration. I began a legal career right out of high school. I participated in what was called co-op. Students would be let out a little early from school and I would go to work at a court reporting firm to practice all I'd learned during school, I loved it! I loved the sense of accomplishment I received when papers shifted from here to there and tasks got accomplished one by one, with visible proof of the progress being made.

In 1992, I moved out of New York to Orlando and quickly found work as a legal secretary. It had long been my vocation in New York yet little did I know that I would take a 50% pay cut due to the relocation. Mom always said, "you pay for the Florida sunshine". I worked for what I understood to be one of the most prestigious law firms in Orlando albeit a small one in the downtown area of Orlando. The senior partner of the firm was a short burly man, with a thick southern accent and snow-white hair, he always reminded me of Santa Claus without the beard. Unfortunately, he didn't have Santa's jovial disposition. This boss was always quite loud and gruff in his communication style and often rough with his employees. He also exhibited behaviors comparable to what you would call discriminatory, especially towards individuals from "up North", "Yankees" he'd call us on occasion. I'd worked for him approximately 7 months or so and my mother at the time either followed me there or helped me secure the position, I can't recall who landed at this unfortunate company first. I had already endured much of his gruff communications for some time and

2

then one day, I was summoned to his office to take dictation, using the exemplary shorthand skills acquired in High School. I finished taking dictation, left his rather impressive office to head into my cubicle where I began transcribing my notes. Shortly thereafter, I returned to his office with the completed letter in hand for his review signature. As I sat across the desk from him, I watched his eyes move from left to right as he read the transcribed letter. I'll never forget the look in his eyes as they glossed over as he suddenly and sternly turned his gaze toward me. He read a few words aloud from the letter with a question in his tone, then, in an aggressive and condescending tone, his heavy southern accent spewed words at me saying, *"theyt's not whuut I sayyd"*. It was loud and he'd just plucked my very last nerve. It was the last straw for me. While I do tend to have quite a high tolerance for such nonsense, I had had enough. In the split second after he finished, I decided I would not put up with his treatment any longer. I knew there was a right way to handle a mistake if I'd made one and that WAS NOT IT. I quickly gathered my stenography notebook and pen from my lap, slowly and calmly I stood up from my chair then... I SLAMMED my notebook down on his desk. Then, in the same thick southern accent that I'd learned to imitate, I replied *"theyt izz whuut you sayyd"*. Now he was the one that looked as startled as I had been just a moment before. For a moment we just stared at each other, I don't think he'd ever been given a taste of his own medicine before. I ended the silence, calmed my anger and voice and said politely said, "You know Mr. So-and-So", (name withheld to protect the guilty), "I don't think this position is for me any longer, I'll be tendering my resignation effective immediately". "Tendering my resignation", I learned those words in high school. Not only did his continuing maltreatment of me reach its pinnacle, but I must also admit that my pride had taken a hit as I was the highest scoring student in my Stenography class at Murray Bertram High School, what I'd transcribed is EXACTLY what he'd said. Little did I know this incident would change the course of my future and my career. After taking stock in my legal career at that point, I did the pros and cons list regarding returning to the legal profession. You see, I had come to the realization that while I enjoyed the administrative function required in legal work, it did not change much from day-to-day. Dictation, dictation, dictation, letters, letters, letters, transcripts, and more transcripts. While the content of it all would change not much else around the administrative aspect changes, if you like consistency then legal administrative work is great, but I needed and embraced change.

I'd come to realize that while I was sitting behind a word processor all day (the PC had not yet advanced), it lacked eyes, ears and a mouth, a person with whom I could communicate and interact, I also needed people in my day to day. This was the part of my strength that was not being utilized to its fullest, I was a people person and knew it. I enjoyed legal reception work earlier in my career but at this point I decided to take my administrative skills into an entirely new occupation. I wasted no time and began to search the newspapers within a few weeks and after an extensive panel interview, I had landed a front desk clerk position for a large hotel management company at one of their airport hotels. Yes, I thought, Front Desk Clerk, I could do that, piece of cake!

Finding myself in a front desk position was an exciting new challenge. No longer did I have to go to work in a stoic office environment. Now I had an opportunity to go to work and walk through the lobby of a prestigious hotel. Little did I know that, across from me at that desk would be some of the most challenging opportunities to problem solve, engage with people from all over the world and still use my administrative skills. It didn't take too long for me to realize that my temperament would be challenged by people from all walks and stages of life. The troubleshooting of major challenges was an adrenaline rush yet I quickly came to realize that being at the end of an angry guest all the time, was not something I wanted as a long-term career choice. I give a lot of credit to those who can endure it over the long term. I also came to realize that the repetitive check in and check out, check in and check out did not change much. Processes didn't change over the 9 months that I had been there and unless new technologies were being implemented which was rare there really wasn't much different in the day-to-day administrative routine. I began to feel as though I still hadn't found an occupation that fulfilled me. I knew I had found my place in hospitality as an industry but I still hadn't found the right role. Nine months into the position, with this realization being so evident, I took the initiative to speak to my Rooms Director who was already earmarking me for front desk supervision. I did not want to lose the opportunity for advanced opportunities but I did need to ensure that the organization was aware of how I believed my talents were being underutilized. The conversation was well received and I joked about my personality not being able to continuously take an environment where I would be yelled at and not be able to defend myself, firmly explain situations or the like because "the guest was always right". We agreed that since I had embedded myself in various committees, my value to the company was noticed and my skills were being utilized further in that way while helping to improve the organization. I was fortunate that the organization was an environment where those contributions were recognized and rewarded with recognition. Within weeks of that conversation, I was advised that the human resources clerk position would be opening due to the resignation of the incumbent human resources administrative assistant. I was thrilled! I had no idea what human resources was but I knew it was an office environment where I typically thrived, I couldn't wait for the opportunity. It would be a few weeks until I started my career in human resources. The perfect mix of people to challenge my personality and ability to communicate with others and paperwork! This time the paperwork and administrative tasks would constantly change and evolve because employment laws always changed and evolved. I believed I had found my niche!

Fundamental Philosophy #2: You Don't Ask You Don't Get

When I went to talk to that Rooms Director, I was demonstrating my belief that you must ask for what you want. No one can read your mind to give you what you want, people need to know about it, you must voice it, ask for it. Take birthdays for example. Year after year you're told to make a wish. So, what do we do, we close our eyes, we hold our breath and we wish for something we want most in the world. Then, we blow out the candle. Exactly how do you expect that wish to come true? I have a proposition for you. On your next birthday, when you're told to make a wish and blow out the candle, leave your eyes open, look around at each and every person in that room and proclaim aloud your wish. You never know who might be in that room to help you manifest it.

If you ask anyone in my personal or professional circles what some of my motto's have been, they might say things like "be fair but firm", "ensure everyone walks out of your office with their dignity intact" and my personal favorite "you don't ask you don't get". It is one of my most favorite because if you don't ask for what you want, then you've given yourself a no answer without asking, why would you set yourself up to fail in this way? You are basically sabotaging yourself. While typically taken out of its true context we've heard people say, "ask and you shall receive". You may not always receive but it certainly doesn't hurt to ask. There have been many opportunities in my life where the simple act of asking for something provided a new opportunity, an opportunity to learn something new, or an opportunity for a new career path or a raise... simply by asking. This is a great way to ensure that the leaders within your organization, the colleagues you work with or the business owners and fellow entrepreneurs around you are aware of what you want, hope for, or need. How can the solution present itself otherwise? Whether that includes advancement or learning opportunities, or a raise, whatever it is, let your dreams, desires and hopes be known. If others don't know, then you are on the journey alone. Your wishes, hopes, dreams and interests won't manifest in the mind of someone who may be able to help you. Let those things be known in your circles and networks. To do it alone casts a single net, widen your net by sharing and asking or informing those around you... it also helps to speak it into existence.

This Fundamental Philosophy would once again manifest later in my career. I was the HR Executive Assistant and had been in HR for 4 years at that point in the same airport hotel. I had just graduated from college and was given the opportunity for a promotion to spearhead the acquisition of a small 190 employee, well-known hotel in Oklahoma City as the Senior Human Resources Manager. Basically, there were no other managers this was the top position of the HR Department of One, it just wasn't going to be a bonus eligible position. That company sure was creative. I decided I would accept the promotion and pursue the opportunity. Within a year or so of my move my mother who also lived in Orlando at this point, was diagnosed with Lymphoma. It's hard to describe how challenging it was to have moved halfway across the country to take on this new opportunity, let alone be helpless to my ailing mom. I focused on my two children getting acclimated to their new surroundings and dove into my work checking in and calling routinely to see how my mom was doing. I blinked and it was months later, the frustration and reality of not being able to be by her side mounted and all the while it was a critical time in my career. I had achieved many accolades within the company after that short first year at that location and had the highest employee opinion survey score in Overall Satisfaction, quite a feat to accomplish during an acquisition of a hotel, I'd been told. Shortly thereafter, the hotel I worked at would be visited by many corporate office leaders who were in town to conduct an employee rally, a foundation of that company's culture. One day during a chat with the communications director of the company, I shared the challenge of my mother's illness and how being so far away made me helpless to attend to her in any way all the while hearing my self-speak *"You don't ask, You don't Get, what do you have to lose.".* I couldn't believe my ears when, within a month I received a call from the Corporate VP of Human Resources indicating there may be an opportunity in Fort Lauderdale. The HR Director position there had been vacant for 6 months and the hotel had been experiencing many challenges. They asked me to consider the position and relocation and interview for the position. "Absolutely", I applied. I interviewed with the executive team and to my answered prayers and delight had been offered the position, I was thrilled!! I arrived in Fort Lauderdale and was now only three hours away from Mom in Orlando! See? You don't ask you don't get...

> If you don't ask for the promotion... you won't get it,
> if you don't ask for the increase in pay... you won't get it,
> if you don't ask if there's money in the budget for training opportunities... you won't get it,
> if you don't ask how you can get your wishes, hopes and dreams met... you won't get,
> if you don't ask you won't get.

I encourage you, as your career and endeavors continue, ASK... you just might get.

Fundamental Philosophy #3: Simple Business Courtesies Matter, Return Phone Calls For Crying out Loud

Management, Leadership and Business in general, requires more than the ability to perform with the knowledge skills and abilities (KSA's) of the role. The most successful, well respected, exemplary managers and leaders possess attributes that are not often written in a job description or covered by the KSA's sought after. Some of these may seem fundamental yet, it does surprise me how often I encounter Senior Leaders and C-Suite Executives that do not possess simple business courtesies. Maybe it's a matter of time management!!, failure to delegate, a reluctance to engage in conflict or maybe it is simply a lack of caring. Whatever the reason, I encourage you as you read these lines to think back regarding whether you may have had opportunities to improve in the area of simple business courtesy and Human Connection.

Over the course of your career, you will or have already received hundreds of phone calls, many of which will be from individuals interested in working with you or for you, you will receive calls from individuals who want to sell you something, you will receive calls from someone who for whatever reason has picked up the phone to call YOU. Every call is an individual saying I'm interested and want to speak with YOU. For some reason YOU ARE IMPORTANT to them you are important enough for them to get over whatever fear they might have of picking up the phone and dialing you. Maybe they had to overcome a fear of rejection in making the call, it took courage for that individual to reach out to you, don't let that rejection come by the discourtesy of simply not taking the time or showing enough respect for their reason for calling by not even returning the call at all. I get it, we are all busy individuals, and I'm not saying that you can't delegate the return call to someone who can gain more insight regarding the reason for the call. But when we return calls to whoever it is that thinks you are important enough to place a call to, it is a sign of mutual respect and a simple business courtesy to return that call, at some point.

Now placing that return call might just put you in a position to have to say that you're not interested in their product or service if that is the reason for their call. It may be a conversation about employing them in whatever it is that they pursued you for but that is a part of the role that you play as a manager, leader, and executive. Being able to say "thank you so much for your interest in working with us; however, at this time we _____" then *fill in your blank*. Maybe your blank is...

...are not looking at new technologies right now, but you can check back in Q3.

...just purchased a solution for that.

...are happy with our current provider but you can send me some information.

And end with, "and I just wanted to give you the courtesy of a return call." Now, if there is an opportunity at some later time to have further conversation regarding whatever it is let them know they can call you in August or November or 2nd Quarter when you review budgets or even that they can give you a call later when you are considering new technologies or whatever it is. Obviously if there truly is no opportunity then you can simply say so and courteously close the door to further conversation. Rarely in my career have I ever found a situation where I closed the door completely to someone interested in doing business with me or my organization. It does happen more often with job candidates (more on that in another chapter) but at the very least I've indicated that I would keep their information on file and then I do so. I keep a digital resource file of information, sales flyers or scanned business cards in the event I, or someone I know, ever need that good or service, I like to say that's the resources part of Human Resources.

Fundamental Philosophy #4: Close the Loop

For me, close the loop means finish what was started and there are dozens of examples but I want to address just a few.

First, close the loop with potential vendors. Part of your responsibility in management is getting things done through others. As a manager and executive, you will encounter times when you must request proposals from organizations that will help you get things done and achieve your goals. You'll obtain bids, compare services, pricing, benefits, and features, and then decide how to proceed. Everyone knows, you can't choose them all, you must select just one typically. So, this means someone or several others will need to be notified they didn't get the opportunity. Some will have the opportunity to work with you, some won't, but all of them should receive the simple business courtesy of you Closing the loop. You started the conversation in some way, close it. Having been on both sides of this dynamic, you must make it a point to ensure you always close the loop. When you reach out to a company and request a proposal, have conversations about the product, features, benefits etc., the other vendor puts in just as much time and effort to go through the processes as you do, if not more. Whether you choose to do business with that company or not, a critical step is to close the loop. Unfortunately, I have seen and experienced situations where managers responsible for this process request information to do business with vendors and then after all the hard work, conversations, negotiations, back and forth... what does the vendor get to show for it?? Crickets... no phone call or even an email that communicates a simple "we've decided on another solution", "we've taken a different direction", "we've delayed our decision", "we won't be proceeding" or whatever the situation. Why not? Part of management and leadership is having to deal with the tougher conversations. When you close the loop, you show you are not averse to having the "We awarded the work to another firm" conversations. It gives you an opportunity to be unique in this regard because unfortunately I've found it to be rare. Yet, those that do it are well respected for it. They stand far above the rest and in some cases can offer valuable feedback and insight to the unsuccessful company that may help that business get better in the future. When you close the loop, you can both move past the proposal process freeing everyone to focus elsewhere.

Second, as a manager you are responsible to ensure not only the success of the things for which you are responsible, but you are also responsible for the success of your employees and colleagues on your team. On occasion those individuals may come to you to help remove barriers in their work, to express concerns over things going on at home or at work or any number of things that you as a manager have a responsibility to address. When an employee comes to you for your help, guidance, coaching, it is your responsibility to close the loop. Never allow an employee's concerns, challenges, or communications to go unanswered or even worse, to go into the proverbial black hole never to be heard from again. In doing so, you risk ruining the trust and confidence of the individuals on your team. When your employees value your relationship enough to bring concerns to you or want to address something with you, you show equal value to that relationship when you do what you can to close the loop and get back to them. Sometimes getting back to them is simply to say you don't have an answer or a resolution yet, but at least Closing the loop in some way keeps them informed until such time as full resolution can be made.

Third, you need to close the loop with job candidates, yes, every single one. Whether an internal and external job candidate, anyone expressing an interest in working with and for you should be given the simple business courtesy of closing the loop regarding their inquiry or application. When someone takes the time to express an interest in working with you or for you, replying to that interest is a simple business courtesy. It does not take much to pick up the phone or send an email or notecard indicating that "we've decided on another candidate." Rarely have I ever had an individual call or email to ask why or engage further. However, in those rare situations, I have shared what they could have done better to improve their chances (more on that in the chapter on interviewing). Nonetheless, getting back to someone to close the loop with candidates is critical. This frees them up to focus and pursue other opportunities and you set an excellent example of respect and courtesy to all who cross your path. You've probably heard "never burn a bridge", when you close the loop and exemplify this simple business courtesy you strengthen that bridge and you never know when your paths may cross again.

If you are not skilled in the art of having these types of conversations which to some people can be tough, reading further will provide more tips tools and insights in this regard.

Fundamental Philosophy #5: Integrity is not a Four-Letter Word.

Merriam Webster defines integrity as: a firm adherence to a code of especially moral or artistic values. Another defines it as: the quality of being honest and having strong moral principles. It is safe to say that we don't all have the same moral standards. Morals are a set of rules that differentiate the right from wrong based on the belief system of society, culture, religion, etc. They can and do vary significantly depending on the region, culture, religion etc. Let me explain further. From the moment that a person is born, they are often told that stealing is bad, being polite is good, offering help is good and being mean is bad. These are examples of morals. Some cultures once stated that the Gods demand a human sacrifice and this was morally acceptable; however other cultures state that killing of any person, under any condition is morally wrong again, MORALS... Values on the other hand are a set of rules that are defined by an individual person. It can be <u>influenced by</u> morals, family, background, upbringing, etc. Values are believed to provide an internal reference for what is good, beneficial, important, useful, beautiful, desirable, constructive, etc. Values are significant to the behavior of a person and determine how the individual will behave. For example, if a person believes that women should be inferior, they will go on to treat women as inferior even if the law stated that men and women are all equal. In many cases, people are so pressured to follow morals that belong to the society, that they disregard their own values. Integrity is a Value and you possess it or not but you can also develop it if you choose, but acting with integrity isn't always easy, sometimes it takes courage. Integrity can be displayed in many ways including honesty, admitting your mistakes, doing what you say you will do, giving credit where it is due, not taking credit for another person's work, standing up for ill treatment of individuals and doing the right thing especially when no one is watching. In Charles Marshall's book entitled, *Shattering the Glass Slipper*, he states "Integrity is doing the right thing when you don't have to—when no one else is looking or will ever know—when there will be no congratulations or recognition for having done so." That's integrity.

I could write for days about the time my manager took credit for my work, the time I knew someone was not being truthful or the time someone didn't do what they'd promised and caused the team to fail, but I could also write about the time I failed at integrity, the grief and guilt compelling me to admit to the biggest mistake of my personal life, and then accepting the dire consequences that would follow. But that is for my next book. What's important for now, is that I learned that whether personally or professionally, integrity is integrity.

As a human and as a manager of people, you will unceasingly be placed in situations when you will have choices relating to your integrity, while you may not always get it right, have the courage to choose integrity. Learn from the times when you may have been unsuccessful in holding to your integrity, using that conviction to spur you on to learning from, and not repeating the failure again.

Fundamental Philosophy #6: Think Outside the Box and Innovate

In the early 2000's, during my tenure as the Director of HR of a world-famous hotel and resort on Miami Beach, and through my involvement with the local Human Resources Association, I was elected its Vice President. As such, I was responsible for securing the location for the monthly meetings but more importantly to select the educational programming. I wanted to ensure that I could provide programming for not only the entry level HR and mid-level professionals, but also ensure advanced programming to address the educational needs of the more tenured human resources professionals.

In my career it has always been my practice to seek out the most accurate source of information, aka get it from the horse's mouth, and I encourage you to do so as well. I had contacts at many Federal, State or Local agencies and wanted to ensure I reached out to those sources for support in this new role. I remember calling my contacts at OSHA (the Occupational Safety and Health Administration), the Equal Employment Opportunity Commission (EEOC) and the Office of Federal Contract Compliance Programs (OFCCP) to ask whether they had anyone who could come and speak at our meetings regarding their regulations, policies, procedures and especially their respective investigation and inspection processes. I thought this was valuable information to provide insight regarding not only how to avoid labor and employment investigations but what to do if the government ever came knocking. It was through these contacts that we delivered great educational programming and we went on to coordinate the first full day Legal Update Conference for that association.

Throughout that experience in selecting the appropriate programming, often service providers would reach out to request an opportunity to speak at our meetings. They included providers of benefit services, employee recognition products and even some retail product providers. Due to some past experiences, while I was certain their presentations would be informational relative to their products and services, I was hesitant because I wanted to ensure they would be educational as well. I didn't want to be responsible for selecting a presenter that might overtake the meeting's educational content with a sales pitch, I've always been bothered by that. Yet, at the same time I wanted to give them an audience with my group since their products and services might be of great value in meeting the needs of our members. Months passed and I didn't know what to do and how to answer this dilemma, after all we only had 12 meetings in the year for speaking opportunities. As the pile of business cards and emails grew and call after call came in, a light bulb finally went on. There was a way that I could provide that opportunity for them to showcase their products and services. What I decided to do was host a Tradeshow during one of our monthly meetings, also the first of its kind for that association. The Trade Show would be paid for in part by exhibitors in the and to ensure every vendor had an opportunity to engage with our members, I created a "Trade Show Passport" so that all attendees would be encouraged to visit every exhibitor in the Tradeshow Hall to get their "passport stamped" giving them a chance to win various raffle prizes we received as donations provided, they had completely stamped passport. While this might be commonplace today, it was a rather unique idea at the time. It was a "win/win" as Stephen Covey would say.

While it might seem a fundamental idea, it had never been done in this association before, I remember the week of being perplexed by this growing list of vendors who wanted an opportunity to meet our members. It was creative thinking, brainstorming and outside of the box thinking that allowed me to discover a solution to the problem. Thinking outside of the box allows for innovation which is something that must always occur to ensure you are staying top in your field, top of your game and top in your managerial skills.

Fundamental Philosophy #7: Never be Afraid to Develop Others or Your Own Replacement

Always have a mentor and be a mentor to others. As you progress in your capacities as a manager and leader it is critical that you surround yourself with people who

- have skills that compliment your own;
- are smarter than you in some areas; and
- you can mentor but also be mentored by.

In so doing, you strengthen yourself. Typically, in my career, I was fortunate to be able to select the individuals on my team or in my department or organization but sometimes I inherited the team. Either way, I always strived to do my best to manage and mentor those around me in some way whether it was a personal or professional mentorship opportunity. Throughout my career as I "climbed the corporate ladder" which sometimes pointed horizontally not vertically, I wanted to ensure those around me had opportunities outside of their respective roles to learn new areas and grow. Often taking someone under my professional wing was the opportunity that presented itself most often. It wasn't until several years into my career that I would work on personal mentorship, but again, that's for the next book. Mentorship does take commitment and time and I used a simple one-on-one "rap session" format. I would document the conversations using a Rap Session form created which you can find in the Appendix of this book. I would meet with each member of my team on a bi-weekly basis for no more than an hour with specific goals. When starting a new role, the conversation might be longer and included learning about my teams past positions, their present position functions, and overview of function procedures, any career path in place or aspired toward the review of any evaluations or reviews, their wish list for themselves both personally and professionally and any professional and personal issues they wanted to share. Thereafter, rap sessions were part of my routine with my team and they included things like asking the respective employee if they had any specific appreciations or recognition for an individual or group that helped them, providing that employee with recognition or appreciation for particular actions and behaviors, asking questions like " Why do we...?" or "Why don't we...?" which created opportunities to discover areas for improvement or better understanding of processes for improvement while also soliciting new ideas. We would discuss their own satisfaction, their career progression, progress on established goals, training opportunities, internal interests, performance concerns, suggestions for improvement or even suggestions for coworkers or feedback for my own improvement as their manager. I would discuss our customer satisfaction issues as well. As managers we have internal customers that include our employees, colleagues, and those we serve and support in our roles. Discussing their wish list which often surfaced needs within the operation or ongoing aspirations for the future. This time would also provide opportunities for status updates on special projects or simply provide a time for me to engage with my team when employee engagement wasn't even being talked about yet. This time permitted an opportunity to proactively check in with them and ascertain if there were any barriers to their progress that I needed to help remove or coach them through removing the barrier themselves. These were true opportunities for mentorship. These rap sessions were an integral part of providing opportunities for individual development, team development and organizational development and improvement. They provided a format for me to check in while also encouraging my team to stretch outside their comfort zones with new projects and initiatives. Whether presenting a new assignment, offering a part in a collaborative project, or simply tasking them with doing something outside their comfort zone or area of specific function, you must always invest in developing others especially those you manage.

Building up and developing those around you also make it possible for you to move on to do other things. When you develop those around you, you may find an individual with the knowledge, skills, and ability to potentially assume your role, even if for a short time. This way you can move on to your next assignment or career aspiration ensuring that you have not left the organization with a shortfall. So often organizations are reluctant to promote or transfer individuals to a new role because it leaves the role being left, vacant. Developing the people around you or even developing your replacement is of huge value to keep you moving forward and those around you moving forward as well.

Fundamental Philosophy #8: You Are Responsible for Your Own Dreams

I believe that each of us is responsible for our own career path whether that be succeeding in the corporate landscape, seeking opportunities outside our own spheres of influence, or transitioning into entrepreneurship, if that is what you desire. The sky is truly the limit and sometimes our dreams are too small. It is up to you to do one thing every day towards achieving the goals and dreams you want in life. What did you do today to achieve a goal or dream you have? We each have our own innate talents, gifts, abilities, and skills but many of them can also be learned to ensure that whatever it is you want to do, you are equally equipped with the skills and abilities that may not be innate, those that must be learned. But it is up to you to pursue them, no one will do it for you.

My journey toward Entrepreneurship started when I was 8 years old with the realization and dream of being a business owner which was instilled in me by my father. As I mentioned before, my father owned a business in Brooklyn, NY, "Brown's Glass Shop." I would come home from school and the bus let me off right in front of Dad's shop. I'll never forget the day my Dad let me answer the phones, *"Brown's Glass Shop, can I help you?"* he'd said to answer. It was the most exciting and proud day of my life. I felt like I was a big girl now... it was then that I knew I would be a business owner one day, just like Dad. This young dream would forever keep me focused on being a business owner. Later, in my early 20's when I lived in the projects of Fort Greene in Brooklyn, NY, during a short period as a stay-at-home mom (only 8 months) I put fliers up at the State University of NY and offered to type up resumes for $20.00 and Term Papers for $5.00 a page. I made some good side money which was so needed as a young mother of two children. The company name was "Type-Right" I did that for a short time, then out of necessity, had to return to full time legal secretarial work. But my dream never wavered. In my early 30's my entrepreneurship dream resurfaced and I tried a few multi-level marketing businesses such as the scrapbooking company Creative Memories (where my love of crafting flourished) and then Amway which was an amazing entrepreneurial training ground. As my hospitality career took off alongside some of those side ventures, I would launch HBL Resources under a different name at the time in 1999. I focused on EEO-1 and Affirmative Action reporting for a large hotel management company. Within about two years I had to put the business on the back burner while my life took some turns and I learned some hard lessons in life. (Did I mention that second book?) As you can see, I never stopped pursuing that dream. I tried different things, succeeded, or failed but still hadn't found the right thing. It didn't stop me from continuing to seek information, resources and training that would give me better and better knowledge, skills, and abilities to continue to pursue my passion of owning a business.

Then in 2011, during my tenure as the VP of HR for another hotel management company, I noticed a shift in the company's cultural philosophies and budget constraints. As a result, seeing an opportunity to practice Fundamental Philosophy #2, I negotiated myself into a part-time VP role, offered to reduce my pay (which helped the company a bit financially) and in the few days I had off, would rebrand, rebuild and re-launch HBL Resources, Inc. to what it is today.

If you have a dream keep pursuing it. If you need or want to learn a new skill and your company won't pay for it, invest in yourself. If you want to be involved in a new project that will teach new skills, request to be involved. If you want to improve your relationships whether inside or outside of work, then it's up to you to do what is necessary to improve them. If you want to be considered for a new opportunity, then apply for it. Then, if you don't get the opportunity to be involved in that new project or you are not given that opportunity you applied for, ask, "why not" then adjust accordingly. This way you can retool to have another opportunity should it come up again. Never accept defeat or setbacks without allowing them to inspire you towards improvement, change, redirection, and determination in some way.

Fundamental Philosophy #9: Learn from "Bad" Managers

I shared my belief that bad managers aren't bad, they are simply untrained in my opinion. However, you can learn just as much from untrained managers as you can from great managers and mentors. You can learn just was much from bad managers as you can from great managers and mentors. Great leadership and managerial acumen can be learned when we experience the negative attitudes, behaviors, inefficiencies, and ineffectiveness of managers who have been placed in the position of management and to whom we must report. These managers may not have ever learned how to manage and ultimately treat employees in their line of supervision. I really don't believe that there are "bad" managers. Believing the best in people, I do believe these same managers are underdeveloped, untrained and unmentored in good managerial qualities and behaviors.

I began to believe that I could learn from bad managers during one long weekend early in my HR career as I navigated adjusting to having a new boss that clearly was an Autocratic leader. I would later value the experience having given me behaviors NOT to model as I later developed into managerial roles. My prior boss and I had gotten along well and the new boss had come in very unexpectedly and suddenly. That was the typical norm for replacing managers, we would call it the "drop ship" manager from the corporate office, often hand selected exclusively for an opportunity, much like I had been for the Oklahoma City and Fort Lauderdale positions I previously wrote about. The first few conversations we had went relatively well and while I seemed to be made to feel like I was not qualified for my own position (after 2 years in the position) I walked out of the office on a Friday determined to make the best of it. I had been in my position about two years, been awarded employee of the month once and felt ready to be challenged and learn more. It was my hope that this new manager would support those aspirations and help me grow to the next level. I later found out I might be wrong. I came back into work on Monday, excited and hopeful just to find that as I began my morning, gathering the piles of paperwork meant for filing, I would be met with a surprise. The file drawers I had habitually used, lined with employee file folders in alphabetical order, no longer contained the employee files that I expected to find. As I searched, drawer after drawer, almost nothing was in the same location as when I had left that previous Friday. One after the other, I looked in familiar places where documents, forms and files were now no longer located. The frustration continued to build as I realized almost 80% of the file drawers' contents had been moved to different locations. What was most upsetting is that the locations of the most used forms files and documents had now been moved to higher drawers. I have never reached a height of even 5 feet; my new manager was quite taller and I later supposed had made all these changes to accommodate her own needs whether height or otherwise. But I was the one who utilized and needed to access those cabinets more often. I was the person responsible for filing, this change now made my job much harder, and it might even take me longer. I was both mad and sad that I was not consulted, advised, or asked to establish a process that would benefit us both. I was not even given the benefit of being advised about the reasons for this drastic change, a change that occurred from one day to another without any notice whatsoever. Thereafter, I aspired never to do that to anyone I would manage or lead. Many might say I succeeded; some might say I failed. What I felt from that experience propelled me to use any negative interactions with a manager as an opportunity to learn what NOT TO DO. It also taught me that a manager and leader, while change is not always easy, a good manager and a solid leader ensures proper management of those changes. Unless the change requires an immediate implementation (such as a risk with regulatory compliance or illegal processes) managers should prepare the organization or team for the change, plan for the change, get feedback and input and hopefully from those who will be affected by the change, implement the changes then review the changes to ensure successful results and modify as needed.

If that experience weren't bad enough, it would also lead to an opportunity to learn first-hand about the frustration associated with the manager who takes credit for your work. While still in my role as HR Executive Assistant, I was a huge fan of and had a knack for spreadsheets. I was determined that no matter what technology I was given to utilize, I would learn to use it in the most advanced applications possible. I would often click around Microsoft applications trying to figure out what this icon did and what that icon did, which helped me learn dozens of things that these software programs could accomplish and that not many of the colleagues in my field knew how to navigate. Since I was a huge fan of spreadsheets (and still am) I remember going through a process in our hotel regarding wage increases for various positions and departments. During budget season we would have to calculate the cost of a percentage increase given across an entire department or for a particular position and the financial impact it would have on the organization.

To this day I still use many of the foundational aspects of that wage scale spreadsheet. During that budget season, it was my director's responsibility to have all the conversations relative to any organizational changes pertaining to the human resources function including benefits and compensation. As I came into the office one day during budget season, I overheard my director speaking to one of the corporate human resources directors about the wage scale changes being recommended and the justification to do so including the organizational changes necessary that were documented and calculated in the spreadsheet. Once the conversation ended relative to that aspect, the corporate director began asking specifically about the wage scale spreadsheet that my director had sent her. I waited to hear her mention me in some respect since I was the person responsible for its development. I took a seat at my desk and began to hear the corporate director asking about the inner workings of the spreadsheet. For at least about 10 minutes of the conversation, there had been no mention of the spreadsheet being developed by me. My heart rate began to rise but I thought of course she would eventually mention it. As my director began to attempt to respond and answer the questions relative to the inner workings of the spreadsheet, it became relatively evident that she had not been the one who built it as she was getting stumped by some of the questions. After one or two more questions, having heard me enter the office, she called me into her office to address the questions. One after the other the corporate director asked me the very same questions my director couldn't answer and of course, having been the creator of the spreadsheet I easily answered all the questions. Questions pertained to the formulas the structure and how the calculations were developed ensuring compliance with the wage and increase policies in effect. They wanted to ensure that the spreadsheet was built on the organizational policies, were accurate in their calculations given variances and that it had maximum reliability. My answers assured them it did. I walked out of the office reassured that the corporate director was now fully aware of whose creation it was. Much to my surprise, the following year the corporate office would introduce my Wage Scale Spreadsheet for use companywide in developing the cost of change calculations needed each budget year. I honestly cannot recall if I was given credit during its company-wide rollout, but what I do know is that, taking credit for someone else's hard work is painful, physically, and emotionally painful to that person. Maybe it was an oversight on my directors part maybe not. I didn't need credit for everything, I still don't but credit stealing when intentional is bad management. When your direct reports achieve you achieve, after all, you likely hired them into your team. Let them flourish and support your goals with their talents and make their contributions known.

Fundamental Philosophy #10: While Change May be Necessary, Forcing it is Not.

Throughout your career you may have opportunities to initiate change, whether it's because policies and processes have changed, or the organization is going in a different direction, change will always be part of your managerial responsibility and managing that change in an effective, efficient way, to maximize productivity, is critical. As we experience change or initiate and manage change, there are some important things to keep in mind, because change is necessary and allows us to continuously improve. While this topic could complete an entire book, I think there are just a few things that require inclusion based on some of my own experiences of both affecting change as well as begin affected by change. I wish I could say that I always used the change management techniques I believe in now but learning and improving how we do things should always be an ongoing process.

During one time of my career, I started as an HR director in a new department. I came in hoping to simply observe how things were being done and why they were being done before I would institute any necessary change, this is a critical part of managing change. To understand why something is done is important to ascertain whether it needs to be changed. One day early in my position, I noticed a staff member faxing off a list naming the individuals who had just attended orientation. Included in the list were things like start date, address, position etcetera, but what was of more concern was the list included the employee's social security number. Where on earth was this list going? When I asked the staff member about the process, she replied it was just "what we've always done". Being an individual who never felt comfortable with that answer, I wanted to ascertain the real reason and began to do some investigating. My research discovered that on the other side of the fax machine was the states worker's compensation board. Certainly, at one point in employment law history, worker's compensation claims information was freely and easily obtained, but at the time of this situation, that process had long since changed making sure employers complied with Americans with Disabilities Act regulations in addition to a myriad of health privacy laws. The bottom line, this process had become illegal. This was obviously a situation where change needed to occur immediately. I explained the situation to the staff, indicated the reasons why the change was necessary and changed it effective immediately, but the involvement and explanation of the why still occurred. Allow me to illustrate further with this anecdote that you may have seen before...

A new bride is making her first big dinner for her husband and tries her hand at her mother's brisket recipe, cutting off the ends of the roast the way her mother always did. Her husband thinks the meat is delicious, but says, "Why do you cut off the ends — that's the best part!" She answers, "That's the way my mother always made it."

The next week, they go to her mother's home and she prepares the famous brisket recipe, again cutting off the ends. The young bride is sure she must be missing some vital information, and asks her mother

"Why do you cut off the ends?" Her mother simply answers, "That's the way my mother always made it."

The next week, they go to the old bubbie's house, and she too prepares the famous brisket recipe, again cutting off the ends. The young bride determined to find the missing link asks her grandma why she cut off the ends. Grandma expressionlessly says, "Darling, that's the only way it will fit in my roasting pan!"

Implementing change can often start with the proverbial "Why do we do what we do?" or "Why do we do what we do, the way we do it?" and is usually more accepted if people are told why the change is necessary and it is usually more supported when people affected by a change are able to participate in making a change. When making changes it is important to understand how it benefits or could be a detriment to the people involved in the change.

CHAPTER 2

INTERVIEWS ARE NOT A ONE-WAY STREET

Having started my hospitality career as a hotel front desk clerk, within 10 years I'd worked my way up to the corporate office as a Director of Recruitment and Succession Planning. It was hard work, taking my own career in my hands and ensuring that my contributions were aligned with the organization's objectives that I believe I was rewarded through a steady stream of promotions and accolades along the way. I thoroughly enjoyed the role and achieved great milestones, but the industry was shifting, mergers and acquisitions abounded and this hotel management company would be affected as well. The corporate office asked for volunteers for a layoff and I raised my hand knowing that many of my colleagues were born and raised in Pittsburgh and that I really didn't care much for the cold winters of Pennsylvania. Those alone made the decision easier.

I accepted a job with the hotel management company that was somewhat involved in the merger and acquisition of my company of 10 years yet six months into that role, Fundamental Philosophy #1: Know When to Pivot To Find Your Passion, showed up again. The company I had transferred to was heavily autocratic[1] in their management style. By now I had become a manager whose style was visionary, democratic, transformational, innovative, and very entrepreneurial. Human Resources Management had become my niche. I had found the right mix of people and paperwork. People to challenge the personality within me including the employees,

---

[1]   Autocratic management is the most top-down approach to management -- employees at the top of the hierarchy hold all the power, making decisions without collaborating or informing their subordinates.

my co-workers, my leaders, and the guest experience. On the "paperwork side", the administrative aspect had never become stagnant, due to ever changing employment law regulations.

All these traits were being smothered in this new company where I was made to feel that I would not be able to bring learned best practices and new ideas to the table. The company seemed to manage human resources from a rigid inflexible box and throughout my tenure there I'd been instructed to "check the Standard Operating Procedure (SOP)" and if there wasn't one that outlined what I needed or wanted to do, then it just couldn't be done. I needed to stay inside the proverbial SOP box; but I'd always been one to "color outside the lines". I realized that I needed an environment where my passion to positively influence the organization would be allowed to survive and thrive. I needed to Pivot again. I desired an organization that could use my developed talents, would welcome new ideas, more efficient processes and allow me to make substantial contributions to the Human Resources function in a more comprehensive way. That passion drove me and I felt ready for the next step in my career, a role where I could freely create or continue to develop the HR infrastructure for the organization. I began to search for just that and found myself applying for the VP of Human Resources at a major limited-service hotel chain. My resume and the telephone interview were enough for them to ask me to come in and interview in person with the Chief Operating Officer at the time.

The Chief Operating Officer, a tall, middle aged, Caucasian gentlemen wore business casual attire and greeted me after his administrative assistant introduced me. We'll call him "Mr. D. I stepped into his large corner office, huge picture windows spanned the size of the room both to my left and directly in front of me. The view was spectacular. A noticed the large high backed executive chair sandwiched between a sizable desk and equally grand credenza. The desk was topped with neat piles of what may have been the projects of his day or maybe even his month all in well-organized piles and his office was neat and orderly. The credenza was lined with a few select family photos and awards strategically placed throughout the office on the desk and bookshelves. He invited me to sit on a comfortable yet firm loveseat as he moved from behind his desk to sit across from me in one of two wing backed chairs, a coffee table between us. He proceeded with the interview beginning to ask about my work history and career up to that point and asking particularly about how I had achieved the many accolades and accomplishments I had achieved thus far. I enjoyed reminiscing about them and all the places my career in hospitality had taken me to that point. I'd started in Orlando, Florida, moved to Oklahoma City, Oklahoma, then Fort Lauderdale, Florida promoted to corporate taking me to Pittsburgh, Pennsylvania and had now landed in Atlanta, Georgia.

It was a pleasant conversation and I believe I did a good job of informing "Mr. D" of my qualifications, accomplishments, and abilities. Then, the interview started to take a slightly serious tone. Looking at me squarely he said, *"So, are you married?"* As loudly as I had ever heard my own inner voice speak, I said to myself, What *did he just ask me? I replied, "Excuse Me?". "I happened to have noticed your ring"* as he motioned toward my left hand, *"...are you married?"* It immediately occurred to me that he had in fact asked me that exact question a moment ago. Various thoughts began to race through my head... *Huh... why would he ask me that? Doesn't he know that's an illegal question? Shouldn't he know he shouldn't ask me that?... Shouldn't he?* Not certain if I should take the opportunity to educate this CEO on the illegal nature of his question I decided to answer, *"Uhm, well, yes, I am"*, obviously the ring on my finger gave that away anyway. Mr. D. followed up with *"...and do you have any children?"* Even more loudly than before my thoughts raced through my head *"What?!? Another illegal question?"* I thought for a moment whether I might be on one of those secret camera TV shows and someone would pop out from behind the desk or credenza with a video camera laughing at the expressions I was making as these questions flew out of his mouth. My mind raced again as I tried to quickly determine if these questions were to test my gumption and chutzpah or my tolerance, especially if he was serious and expected real responses. *He's the CEO for Crying out Loud! How does he not know -- at this level of his career—that he's asking me illegal questions or maybe he simply doesn't care.* Noticeably uncomfortable now, I went along with the line of questioning for the interview and replied *"Yes, I do, but excuse me, I'm not sure how that is relevant to the job for which I'm applying?"*, my professional tone and verbiage catching him a bit by surprise. Hoping this reply would jar him back into the reality of the situation, he replied with a somewhat perturbed and matter of fact chuckle, *"well, I'm just trying to determine if childcare arrangements need to be taken care of to ensure you can work the extensive hours that may be required of this position?"* There was my inner voice again, *Am I in the twilight zone!? Did I just time travel back to the 1950's when this line of questioning was acceptable?* That was it... in seconds, my mind was made up that he was NOT looking to see if I would correct him, but he was truly asking illegal questions that had no bearing on my ability to perform the job. Not only did Mr. D. seem to have no knowledge or understanding that he had been asking me illegal questions, if he was aware, he showed no concern in doing so whatsoever. I decided on a textbook HR answer, *"There's nothing that would prohibit me from completing the essential functions and working the hours required of this position."* By then I had already decided that I wouldn't be working for him or with him in this organization.

My mind was unrelenting... *"This is outrageous, If he doesn't know he's asking me illegal questions or doesn't care, I could sue him for asking them. If I take this job, I'll have to educate him. If he does know, then do I REALLY want an uphill battle with this CEO who is making no bones about his ability to ask these questions or the risk he is taking in asking them? Is this a role I choose to put myself in at this stage of my career?"* All of that flashed through my mind. I could hear myself testify in court, *"Uhm, well your honor...yes Mr. D. has been known to ask inappropriate interview questions".* I stepped up to that plate a time or two earlier in my career; but did I really want to do it again with a C-Suite CEO who was seemingly uneducated at this level or clearly had no respect for employment law? NOPE! I was not going to work at this company and I was going to leave this interview on my own terms.

"So, do you have any questions for me?" Mr. D. asked. I had come prepared with my list of questions. Questions about the company's Mission, Vision, Values..., why was the position open..., what would be the traits needed for success in the position... and many more. I had come into this interview wanting this job and was prepared to secure this position as I had in the past when I wanted a role. To that point in my career there was never an opportunity that I'd interviewed for that I wasn't offered. I had had a wonderfully rewarding career. Yet, I proceeded to intentionally bomb the rest of the interview and was determined to have fun doing it!

"Well, yes I do." I paused for affect, *"What a lovely picture you have on your credenza, is that your family?"*, Mr. D. looks behind him to the family photo on his credenza, *"Yes it i..."*. I quickly interrupted, So *are you married too, is that your lovely wife in the photo?"*, *"Yes, that's my family,"* he answered, a disapproving look on his face suddenly emerged. *"Your children are beautiful, I would imagine you, too, have taken care of any childcare arrangements necessary for you to be here today as well?"* The disapproving look turned into a contemptuous grimace on his face. I had made my point clear. *"I have no further questions"* I replied, trying to sound like some of the attorneys I had worked with in my past. A few added words were exchanged about the interview process and when they'd be making decisions, but I paid no attention. This was not the role for me and I had visions of suing their pants off. Not just because of the illegal questions but especially if they hired a male, a single male with no children! I'm sure I wasn't the first married female with children who might have been overlooked for a job at this hotelier or the countless others, hospitality leadership was a very male dominated industry in the 90's and in some ways still is. Employers and managers be warned, you are equally as culpable as your organization when breaking certain employment laws. I left that interview knowing that I would further resolve to ensure managers were trained to know the importance of all the employment laws and tell them of their individual risk in asking such questions of their candidates, regardless of gender or otherwise.

Legal Interviewing

Understanding current laws and guidelines governing hiring practices is a critical component of your managerial responsibility. Preparing for an interview to ensure a thorough, legal, and appropriate interview is conducted is your role as a manager. Questions should be focused on work related knowledge, skills and abilities that help you gauge a candidate's fit for a particular position based on their knowledge, and on their skills and proven abilities.

During employment interviews certain questions are considered discriminatory and therefore, unlawful to ask during the pre-employment interview process. Take a moment to answer this brief quiz and indicate if you think the question is lawful and permitted to be asked during a pre-employment interview, discriminatory and should not be asked during the interview or if you are not sure. Complete the chart but keep in mind, the goal is to gauge what you know now, so don't worry about what you may not be aware of at this time.

Inquiry	Lawful	Discriminatory	Not Sure
1. Asking if a candidate has ever worked under another name.			
2. Asking a candidate where they are from or their birthplace.			
3. Asking for birthplace of applicant's parents, spouse, or other relatives.			
4. Asking a candidate to submit proof of age by supplying birth certificate if required to support alcoholic beverage, minimum age requirements.			
5. Asking a candidate for religious affiliation, name of church, parish, or religious holidays observed for scheduling purposes.			

6. Asking a candidate if they are a citizen of the U.S.			
7. Asking a candidate for date of citizenship acquisition.			
8. Asking a candidate if they were ever arrested and to indicate the reason.			
9. Asking a candidate to indicate what foreign languages can be read, written, or spoken fluently.			
10. Asking a candidate how their language ability was acquired to read, write, or speak a foreign language.			
11. Asking a candidate about previous work experience.			
12. Asking a candidate regarding the specifics regarding why they were terminated if listed as a reason for leaving previous jobs.			
13. Requesting candidate to provide names of family or relatives who also work in the company.			
14. Asking a female candidate for her maiden name.			
15. Asking for names of clubs and societies in which membership is held.			

You can obtain the answer key outlining questions that are acceptable and unacceptable in The CMM Supplemental Workbook & Toolkit via download at https://thecompletemanagermakeover. com/thecmm/cmm-supplemental-toolkit/. Think about what you already know or may have heard regarding the various attributes and characteristics that are protected by law? While the list continues to grow as new legislations are enacted, there are many laws that regulate pre-employment processes.

The Civil Rights Act of 1964 is also known as Title VII and was a groundbreaking civil rights and labor law enacted in the United States that barred discrimination based on race, color, religion, sex, or national origin. What many don't easily recall is that Title VII also prohibited unequal application of voter registration requirements, and racial segregation in schools, employment, and public accommodations. Some states, cities, or even municipalities recognize additional protected characteristics such as sexual orientation, sexual identity, victims of domestic violence, gender identity, gender and marital status, and the list continues to grow. In 1978, Title VII was amended to clarify that candidates or employee with a pregnancy or related condition must be treated the same as other candidates and employees based on their eligibility and/or inability to work. In 1986, the United States Supreme Court first ruled that sexual harassment in the workplace also violated Title VII under its gender category. Throughout the years we have seen these laws and protected characteristics broadened as litigation continues to shape their interpretation and application in the workplace.

Another Preemployment and Post-Employment law to consider in the workplace is the Americans with Disabilities Act also known as ADA. The ADA protects individuals who have a disability which is defined as a physical or mental impairment that substantially limits one or more major life activities. Think for a moment about what you would consider your major life activities? While most of us would consider the obvious physical impairments possibly limiting one or more of our five senses like being blind/vision impaired, deaf, or hearing impaired, being unable to walk or speak, mental impairments are also included as disabilities and these are much more difficult to detect. These may include things such as panic disorders, major depressions, dipolar disorders, and the list goes on. Care must be taken during the interview process to ensure that questions being asked don't trip Title VII, or ADA regulations. As an interviewing representative, your responsibility to your organization is to ensure you don't ask questions that would be considered illegal under these and many other laws causing potential litigation.

There is much more to consider regarding your responsibility as a manager as we discuss individuals with a disability. Would you think that a candidate is covered under the ADA if a current employee told you that the candidate was his friend, and that he might have difficulty hearing you because he was partially hearing impaired? It may surprise you to know that the candidate would be covered due to that disclosure of the disability because the friend advised you which would lead to a record of the impairment.

There are several other laws to consider including Pay discrimination among females which has received much publicity in the past decade and still exists in many companies. The Equal Pay Act was enacted in 1963 and prohibits gender-based wage discrimination and others that govern both pre- and post-employment including the Age Discrimination in Employment Act. This law protects workers who are over 40 years old. It is because of these laws and many others that certain questions are considered discriminatory during the pre-employment interview process but there is much more regarding federal employment laws in a future chapter.

The pre-employment and interview process is further regulated by an act called Uniform Guidelines of Employee Selection Procedures enacted in 1978, also known as UGESP. This act prohibits employers' selection policies and practices from having an adverse impact[2] on the employment opportunities for any race, sex, or ethnic group unless it is a business necessity. These things include a procedure such as the advertising of gender specific positions such as "Hostess only" when both males and females can perform the job, it also includes prohibiting the

---

[2] An unwanted and unanticipated result of taking a particular action. In the context of business employment decisions, an adverse impact refers to a disparity in selection for hiring or promotion that disadvantages individuals of a particular race, ethnicity or sex.
Read more: http://www.businessdictionary.com/definition/adverse-impact.html

development of procedures that would exclude specific races, genders, and ethnic groups such as looking for specific groups unless required by the position, like in the example of a Ladies or Men's Restroom Attendant. This is where a gender specific hire would be required and legal.

Hiring Processes

Now that we know a bit about what questions can and can't be asked from a legal perspective, the hiring process can vary from company to company but may include one or more of the following steps:

1. **Open a Requisition to fill a position.** This is typically a step required for much larger organizations that need to ensure hiring is controlled and conducted only for positions that have become open due to employee's leaving or transferring to another role or the approval to add to the staffing levels.
2. **Post the Position internally and externally.** This is done by creating a written or digital job posting and sometimes a marketing piece that outlines the availability of the position and the method by which individuals can apply for the job. Today, Job posting is often done digitally through online job boards. Posting the information both internally and externally helps to ensure the organization gives opportunity to both internal candidates who may be interested in the role but also to advise external candidates of the opening should there be no qualified internal candidates. While job posting is not a legal requirement for private sector employers, it is viewed favorably by the Equal Employment Opportunity Commission (EEOC) and is considered a best practice since it helps to reduce any perceptions of discriminatory hiring practices. As a well-rounded manager you should ensure that you can support your own recruitment efforts by contacting your own sources as well through networking with colleagues or industry specific associations. It is every manager's responsibility to

support overall recruitment efforts. Some additional external recruitment sources should include but may not be limited to:

- Colleges
- Community Education School
- Specialty Schools (such as Culinary)
- High Schools
- Internet Job Sites
- Local Job Agencies
- Local Publications (Employment Guides)
- Minority Recruitment Sources
- One Stop Center (Unemployment Office)
- Technical/Vocational Schools
- Veterans Organizations

3. **Application Process.** Whether a manual system or digital, it's important that the application be complete, and no areas are left blank. If a candidate submits an online or paper application with blanks, it's ok to return it and politely ask that any missing information be completed. Be sure there is a way for candidates to sign and date the application. A few more things to consider especially if you are still using paper applications is to ensure the respective areas are completed with specific answers such as indicating See Resume or Indicating Negotiable for salary expectations. It is important to never write or take notes on an employment application, instead I recommend use of an applicant/interview screening form to capture responses and notes from an interview, more on that later. You can find a sample applicant screening form in The CMM Supplemental Workbook & Toolkit via download at https://thecompletemanagermakeover.com/thecmm/cmm-supplemental-toolkit/. You will want to look for specific things on the application such as the position applied for, expected range of pay, desired hours, skills they bring to the position, reasons for leaving previous positions and especially any gaps in employment. By reviewing these areas prior to the interview, you will be able to focus interview

questions around needed information and maximize the time with the applicant. You also want to ensure all spaces on an application are completed by the candidate, this way you limit the possibility of information being filled in by another person or later. The screening form, because it is standardized provides a consistent format to capture pertinent information and reduce the perception of subjectivity.

4. **Screening of Candidates.** Screening consists of asking pre-qualifying questions to ensure the candidate possesses the necessary knowledge, skills, and abilities to accomplish the job for which they are applying. Often, with today's digital age and online application processes, screening can be done with application software in the various online job boards that exist, which also becomes a way for organizations to comply with candidate tracking, a recordkeeping requirement.

5. **Candidate Interviews.** Once candidates have been screened and potential candidates are selected from the numerous individuals who have applied, formal interviews then take place. This can be done virtually with Video Conferencing software or in person depending on the preference of the interviewers or the organizations internal processes. Documenting the conversation using the Applicant Screening Form is highly recommended to formally document the discussion and the information learned during the interview. This provides you and the employer with information regarding the reasons why you chose to hire or not to hire an applicant. This information can be critical should the employer ever be accused of pre-employment discriminatory practices based on any of the pre-employment regulations. Caution should be taken in ensuring all notes are job related and are not discriminatory in any way, such as writing if the candidate disclosed that they were married or had children etc. It is believed that if a hiring manager had the information, it could certainly have been used in making employment or hiring decisions. As managers we must be cognizant of our conscious and unconscious biases ensuring we are not allowing them to hinder an objective hiring decision.

6. **Decision to Hire or Not.** Once the interviews are conducted, a decision to hire is made. In some cases, it may require more than one interview, involve an internal HR representative. department representative, panel interview or senior manager. Sometimes it might be all of them. Communicating the hiring decision should be made by the human resources representative or the designated department or representative.

7. **Background Check and/or Drug Testing.** Some organizations conduct pre-employment assessments, background checks and/or drug testing the latter of which are highly regulated by the Fair Credit Reporting Act of 1970 (FCRA). The FCRA defines an employees' and potential employees' rights regarding how employers use information obtained from reports compiled by third party credit reporting agencies especially when used as the basis for employment decisions. The FCRA, among other things, requires that candidates pre-authorize the discovery of their background information, are advised of their rights in the process, are given an opportunity to correct inaccurate information and are advised of any adverse action that is taken because of the information contained within the reports provided to employers. This is a detailed process to ensure the applicants rights are adhered to when making employment decisions especially if made adversely due to the disclosure of information contained in the reports.

8. **The Hire.** If a candidate is chosen to be hired, an offer of employment is then made which should include as many details of the position as possible to ensure transparency, clarity and ensure no prior miscommunications have occurred during the pre-employment process. Caution should be taken to make a verbal offer indicating the position for which they've been hired, the rate of pay that they would be accepting, the general hours of employment, and any other relevant information regarding benefits and compensation. Just like you have made the decision whether to hire a candidate or not, the candidate must also decide whether to join your organization.

You've already read about one of my worst interviews, do you have a story like that? While I certainly hope not, I'm sure that you might and that is exactly what we want to avoid as a trained and effective manager. Keep in mind that with today's workforce, candidates are Interviewing YOU just as much as YOU are Interviewing THEM. I want to provide a different perspective on how you should approach the interview process. I wrote *Guest Satisfaction – Another Perspective* during my tenure as a Director of Human Resources at the Fontainebleau on Miami Beach. We were having quite the struggle with managers being late or canceling interviews at the last minute and I wanted to give them a healthy view because this was not acceptable and hurting our reputation in the workplace and marketplace. If you are a hiring manager or have any part in hiring process, I hope you will consider this perspective when conducting your recruitment functions.

Customer Satisfaction – Another Perspective

We all have customers or are customers at one time or another. If you want your business to be successful you must agree with the perspective that our customers are #1 and should be treated with friendly hospitality, professionalism, and prompt attention.

When customers are made to feel unwelcome or are not attended to promptly, what is the result? They do not return, hence a negative reflection on both the respective department and the company. We must also remember that this customer experience can be shared by word of mouth and now an even wider readership with the ever-growing social media platforms to which many of us now have access. Based on various American Express Customer Service Surveys, one-third of consumers say they would consider switching companies after just one instance of bad customer service and Zendesk recently reported that 95% of customers tell others about a bad experience.

Managers, Leaders and Human Resources professionals alike have another kind of 'customer' to serve. They are not looking for a product or service or value for price paid. They are looking for employment, a means by which to obtain those things. They are looking for a career and they will encounter a "customer" experience on that journey. As 'customers' candidates should be treated just as any other customer of your company. They should be treated with <u>friendly hospitality, professionalism, and prompt attention</u>. If prospective employees are not treated in this manner, you run the risk of losing your next star, dedicated employee, or even senior leader. Just like customers will share their poor experiences, so will and should candidates. They will tell their friends about the lack of response from your company, lack of a returned phone call when promised or the length of time they waited for you to meet with them at their appointed time. They will share how you treated them during the interview process or how you ghosted them after several interviews because you lacked the courtesy and _____ to advise them that "...at this time another candidate was selected". (Fill in your own blank.)

You may think there are plenty of candidates out there, but the candidate with the skills and qualifications you are seeking may have just heard about the bad experience your less qualified candidate had, and they just might tell two friends, and they'll tell two friends and so on and so on and so on... They will say "Oh... you don't want to work there; they don't treat job candidates very well so they probably don't treat their employees any differently!"

41

So, when you get that opportunity to meet with a candidate that may well be your next employee, don't view it as a burden or chore but think of that candidate just as seriously or importantly as you would that potential customer, guest, or client. After all, it is truly about finding that special "customer" that will help you attend to your special customers and clients.

Hire the FIT, Train the Skill

There are several tools and assessments on the market that will help you hire the right person for your organization. My firm offers the Hiring Insights DISC Assessment[3] through our partner, Personality Insights®. They can be found here: https://thecompletemanagermakeover.com/d-i-s-c-assessments. While this tool has been invaluable for many of my clients, I never recommend it as the ONLY way to assess a candidate's FIT for your organization, but it certainly provides an added level of surety for the hire.

I still believe that a legal, efficient, and effective interview is one of the best ways to make that final determination and even then, sometimes, like Forrest Gump says, "you never know what you're gonna get". Nonetheless, the more efficient your interview process, questioning techniques and rapport building skills are during that interview, the better insight you will have to formulate your decision.

---

[3]   Hiring Insights DISC Assessments and tools are a simple way to find candidates that "FIT" a particular job or position that you are trying to fill. When you find a candidate that "fits," then he or she will naturally excel in their work environment.

Most hiring processes rely heavily on looking at skills and qualifications - which is necessary. Hiring Insights provides an added way for you to ENHANCE your ability to find people who are likely to perform well AND remain happy at work or on your team. The result? Turnover is reduced and people stay longer - which saves you time and money.

The P.R.I.D.E.S. Model™

To provide a framework for managers and supervisors to conduct a professional interview and make it easier to identify the best candidate for a position, I have developed a six-step interview model which is called the *P.R.I.D.E.S. Model of Interviewing™*. My goal is that it will be used by a manager or supervisor who P.R.I.D.E.S. themselves in the interview process. Remember the purpose of the interview is to create a positive and professional association between both of you, obtain enough information from the candidate to make an objective decision about their ability to perform the job, inform the candidate about the specifics of the position, provide insight about your company, and get enough information for both of you to make a decision regarding whether to consider a mutually beneficial employment relationship.

The P.R.I.D.E.S. Model of Interviewing™ was developed for use during the final candidate phase of interviewing which can be accomplished in person or virtually although I always recommend a face-to-face at some point in the interview process. It may seem like a lengthy process and often to ensure all steps in our model are accomplished you might schedule a conversation for a minimum of 45 minutes; however, I use this exact same model during a 20-30-minute telephone pre-screening interview when necessary. It is important that the process is thorough and professional from beginning to end and that during the interview, all the steps are accomplished in the order outlined to ensure the most effective outcome.

You will need an applicant screening form or other way of capturing notes, which helps document specific answers, any thoughts you have about the candidate relating to job applicability and becomes a great source of information if you ever need to recall any part of the interview later after hire. Remember that your notes should include only legally acceptable comments such as answers to a candidates hours availability, schedule restrictions, predetermined vacations, or answers to questions regarding the candidates knowledge, skills, and abilities.

So, let's review the steps.

Step 1: Prepare for the Interview

Proper interview techniques begin with careful preparation. A careful review of several things will help point out areas to explore further on in the interview. Preparing for the interview consists of reviewing the employment application, resume, job description, job specific details such as hours, pay and general benefit information, or company specific information that you may want to share with a candidate about the organization. Here are a few items you want to review and why:

- Employment Application/Resume: As previously mentioned you are looking for things that are either consistent or inconsistent with the job responsibilities and requirements for which you are hiring. Gaps in employment, missing information, red flag items like reasons for termination should be discussed during the interview to ensure there is nothing left out. A resume can provide insight into the kind of work your candidate has done previously, but you should not take what is written down at face value, be prepared to ask about it. Asking questions about how someone achieved a certain increase or decrease in performance goals, what steps they took to achieve their accolades and how they managed a team project to stay on budget or timeline are important things to ask. This can provide insight into whether they managed the project and were an integral part of the accomplishment or if they were merely one part of the larger scope of work. Reviewing the resume in this way helps you to prepare those specific questions in advance.
- Job Descriptions and Performance Objectives: It is common to assume that we know every aspect of the job for which we've been tasked to hire. Reviewing the job description and understanding the performance outcomes and objectives is always helpful to be reminded of the job duties, knowledge, skills, and abilities that may

sometimes be forgotten. A brief review ensures awareness of other items you might want to touch upon during the conversation. Knowing the job requirements helps to prepare specific questions focused on the candidates past experiences relative to those various duties and requirements.

- Company Culture and Values: You may think you have a great grip on the company's culture, mission vision and values or brand promise but if you had to write down the answer to "What is your company's mission?", could you do it right now? Reviewing the company culture mission, vision, values, or brand promise helps you keep it top of mind but also helps you stay focused on asking your candidate the right questions to determine if they are aligned with your company's culture as well. Ensuring cultural alignment and hiring based on alignment of your company's culture, values and beliefs helps to improve the probability of employee retention.

- Preparation of Questions: Once you have reviewed the pertinent documents, you likely have begun to prepare the questions you would like to discuss. I recommend that you ask the same core questions of all final candidates, leaving room for individualized questions based on everyone's experiences and resume. You should pay particularly close attention to items on the resume that detail specific accomplishments. An example might be "Increased revenues by 10%" or "Decreased expenses by 15% year over year". These are items on a resume where I like to really dig. If they list an accomplishment, then they should be able to articulate exactly how they achieved it and I'll ask about the process in its entirety and what part they especially played in the achievement. Many a candidate across the desk from me has been stumped when asked exactly how they accomplished their achievements and accolades. I also like to ask about their awards and accolades and what they believe attributed to the recognition. people don't always get an opportunity to talk about their accomplishments and what they believe they did to receive them. I like to hear about what they did in their organization that resulted in the recognition or award. It also serves as an opportunity to hear about some of the projects they worked on, teams they lead or innovative ideas they implemented.

We have often heard that past behavior tends to be a predictor of future performance, but I say, it depends. While I do still use some of the foundational principles of the behavioral based interview model, since candidates can be easily coached to success, I also ask follow-up questions to get the thorough details of the broader answer and a common follow-up question is "What would you do differently?" or "What did you learn from it". In additional to drilling down further, I like to formulate my questions with a similar structure as the SMART Goal (see page _____. The use of a SMART Goal that ties to behavior and accomplishing performance expectations might look like this for an Executive Chef, "One of the skills required in this role is to ensure the food cost remains at or under 30% while maintaining food quality. What are some specific ways you have controlled food cost that didn't have a negative impact on quality? BOOM!! If they cannot speak to processes such as inventory management, recipe costing, portion control, purchasing processes and the like, they may not be the best person for the job. (To all the great F&B Managers and Executive Chefs I worked with, YES, I paid attention.)

While asking the candidate to tell you about a specific experience is a great way to gauge how they may handle various situations and job functions, asking about the specifics of their ability to perform and achieve quantifiable results is another. Developing questions like this will help you determine the type of potential behaviors and skill sets you want to hear about from the candidate. Questions focused on behavioral and skill-based examples relating to past jobs and/or school experiences are helpful. These interview questions and their follow-up questions may look something like this:

1. Describe a time when you were faced with a stressful situation, what was the stressor how did you manage it?
    a. What would you have done differently?
    b. What did you learn from that experience?

2. Tell me about a recent situation in which you had to deal with an angry customer or guest?
    a. What was the result?
    b. In hindsight, what else could you have done?

3. Our guest services scores are currently below average. What are some of the strategies you have implemented in the past to improve guest satisfaction?
    a. How did you determine the strategy to implement?
    b. Was there a quantifiable change in the guest service scores? Why/Why Not?

4. Tell me about a time when you had too many things to accomplish and it was evident a deadline would not be met? What did you do?
    a. Would you do anything differently if it had occurred today?

Notice the initial question does not give the hint of a desired result which has often been the misstep of behavior-based interview questions. For example, a candidate would easily know how to answer this modified question based on example #2 above.

Tell me about a recent situation in which you had to deal with an upset customer or guest? How did you calm the situation?

In this example, the candidate will go to an example when they were able to calm the guest. The question outlined in #2 above gives no specific outcome, only that the candidate had to deal with an upset guest. The candidate could select a time when they were unable to calm the guest or one where they were not, the selection is up to them. The follow-up questions allow you to gauge the candidate's thought process, strategic reasoning, ability to learn from past experiences and apply new levels of learning to past experiences. These types of open-ended questions steer the candidate to the information you need to collect and encourage the candidate to talk. Broad based questions should be used to open the discussion and collect information required to make hiring decisions.

Once your questions are ready, the next step in preparation is to locate a comfortable private setting. There's nothing wrong with a local coffee shop so long as there is some semblance of privacy. Nothing is worse than having an interview at a location where people are coming and going or it's extremely distracting. Make sure that your phone calls are forwarded to voicemail or the phone is placed on silent, every effort should be made to ensure that there are no interruptions during your interview. Remember the person in front of you should be treated as your guest, your customer. If there is a call that you absolutely must take, there is nothing wrong with advising the candidate of that in advance during the rapport building step which is next. Make certain that you have reviewed the application in advance, have your questions planned and allow ample time for the interview. Be sure you are also on time for the interview, being late to an interview, that YOU scheduled, leads the candidate to believe that promptness is not important to you or the company or that you don't consider their time just as valuable as your own.

Step 2: Rapport Building

If you have ever been interviewed, then you know how stressful it can be. Building rapport is essential so that your candidate is at ease and settled in comfortably for a thorough conversation. Upon first meeting your candidate obviously you want to sincerely welcome them and thank them for taking the time. Time is limited for all of us, they have taken time out of their life, just like you have taken time out of yours. Rapport building should take no more than five or so minutes and small talk should be used to settle them into the interview. Questions about the weather or "Did you find the office/coffee shop ok?" or "How was your trip here" help create a casual setting providing stress-free rapport building conversation. Be natural and relaxed, but remain professional, show interest in the candidate as a prospective employee but also as a person. Have you ever been made to feel as though someone was only interested in what they could get from you? Don't be that person. Don't rush or make the candidate feel like they are being glossed over. Since you most likely will be taking notes during the interview and using your screening form, advise the candidate that you may be taking notes. I always like to say, "I'll be taking notes because I speak to a lot of candidates and it's important for me to remember our unique and individual conversation". This will put the candidate at ease about your note taking and help you remember key information, highlights or concerns and indicates to the candidate that the information they are sharing is important.

There are two things that can occur during rapport building that can influence your opinion about a candidate, without you really having all the facts yet. They are the Halo Effect and the Horns Effect. The term "halo effect" and "horns effect" were first presented in a 1920 paper authored by Edward Thorndike titled "A Constant Error in Psychological Ratings." The **Halo effect** is when you attribute positive qualities to a person based on a few known positive qualities. The one or two good aspects of a candidate make them look good in most other areas as well and often occurs when commonalities are found with a candidate. Maybe you both grew up in the same place, know the same people, like the same sports teams or they are wearing your favorite color. You wind up hiring a friend with common likes and dislikes when what you needed was an administrative assistant who could ensure office organization, timely project management and efficient typing skills.

Then there is the **Horns effect** which is when you attribute negative qualities to a person based on one or two known qualities. This occurs when a negative perception is generalized to other aspects of the candidate. A typical horns effect may occur when the candidate has a sweaty palm during a nervous handshake, they might be wearing a perfume or cologne that is not agreeable to you or they discussed something for which you have a negative association. These effects might have you overlooking a candidate who is otherwise qualified for the job. With either the Halo effect or horns effect, one generalization can make the best candidate, a wrong candidate, when they really are the right candidate!

Being aware of these effects help us to remain as objective as possible to safeguard that we do not make judgments on one trait without having considered the whole picture. As an interviewer, you must do your best to acknowledge your personal biases and remove them. Don't let the candidate perceive approval or disapproval from you and be aware of your body language responses and other non-verbal cues so that does not get infused into the conversation.

Step 3: *Information Gathering*

This step should comprise the bulk of your interview time and is the most important section of the interview. Using the application, your screening form, and your prepared questions as a guide, as mentioned, you should ask similar questions of each candidate to allow for easy comparison. The 80/20 rule says the candidate should talk 80% of the time and you, as the interviewer, should talk 20% of the time. Again, asking broad based open-ended and behavior-based questions and be sure to ask any follow-up questions. Follow-up questions draw on the candidate's prior response to encourage him/her to share more details or feelings. Probe by saying "Tell me more about that" or "How did you react in that situation?" or simply, "Why?". Do not accept general answers and probe for more specific information.

Some candidates will share too much information or get off track. Tactfully redirecting these candidate helps you get them back to the more relevant conversation. An example of redirecting is "Sounds like you really enjoyed rock climbing, Joe, I would love to hear more about the job you had that summer." Then ask your next question.

Do not lose eye contact for long periods of time by taking extensive notes, as it can be distracting to the applicant. Your role is to listen carefully for the true meaning of what the candidate is saying. Be attentive and practice active listening skills. Remember that silence can be golden. Care should be taken when probing for negative information. If there is more to be said by the candidate on an issue, pause and look at the candidate for several seconds. Do not continue to talk if the candidate does not reply quickly. Silences are okay and may occur if the candidate needs time to think. This technique can often lead to the most revealing information.

Reinforce the applicant's answers by nodding, smiling, etc., before moving to the next step of the interview. You can always close your section of the questioning by asking if there is anything else that you should know about them. This will get the candidate to share information that you have not discussed but which may be important to your decision.

You can find an extensive list of behavior-based interview questions relating to customer service, effective communication, judgment, learning ability, experience, education and more in the Appendix.

Step 4: Describe the Position and Company

When the information gathering portion of the interview is concluded, the next step in the process is to describe the position and the company in more detail. Describe the position completely and honestly. While the job duties may have been reviewed previously, briefly explain the job duties and responsibilities, who the individual will report to if not you, discuss the hours of the position and the general schedule and any other pertinent information. It is an important step to also communicate the rate or range of pay period even though it may have been previously posted or included in the application process. Now is a good time to reiterate this information to ensure there is still alignment needed with salary expectations. If it's a high pace environment, let them know that it's ok to discuss the great parts of the job as well as the areas that may provide personal and professional challenges. The more accurate a job preview you can provide, the better able you are to hire the right person who completely understands the big picture of the role. If you have enough time, share the reasons why you think your company is a great company to work with.

Discussing the company's culture, mission, vision, and values is important and often in my information gathering I ask what the candidate knows about the company hoping to hear what homework they have done. Cover general performance expectations and it may be appropriate to show the candidate the work area so consider giving a tour of the workplace. It's ok to let them experience the environment first-hand and what their workspace, office or desk might look like, be sure to advise them that you do this with all candidates to prevent them from thinking they already have the job.

If you do have an opportunity to walk them around the location, the tour also serves as a great opportunity for you to observe the verbal and non-verbal interaction they may have with others in the workplace such as potential co-workers. Do they smile and engage with others in the workplace or are they aloof and standoffish? Making a mental note of these behaviors is important in ensuring you have the right fit for the role. It may also be appropriate to introduce the candidate to current employees or other key managers, doing so by simply introducing them as a prospective candidate. These interactions can also be helpful to the candidate in making an informed decision for themselves regarding the possibility of joining the company. Not all roles require an outgoing personality, maybe the position requires self-sufficiency, but we will cover that in a future chapter regarding the

Be sure to make time to share information about the history of the company, how it supports volunteerism, corporate sustainability, or corporate responsibility, which is highly sought after at companies in today's workforce.

Finally, cover key company benefits, not just medical, dental and life insurances but tell the candidate about the holidays the company recognizes, vacation schedule, volunteer days or other special programs that might be of interest to them. You are responsible to know at least general information about the various employee benefits so that you can describe them and answer the candidates' questions adequately. However, if you don't know, don't guess, advise the candidate that you will get back to them with an answer or make a quick call prior to the close of the interview process to get the information before the candidate leaves. Remember, they are deciding about you and your company too. On occasion, I've even shared a copy of the company newsletter or sent one digitally after the interview was completed.

Step 5: Expect and Ask for Questions

Next, ask if the candidate if they have any questions for you. It is likely that you were so thorough in describing the position and the company that you may have already answered most of their questions. Questions a candidate asks can provide knowledge about their interest and motivation in working for you and your company. It is also important in this phase to ensure that the candidate has as much information as they need to decide about the position should you decide to proceed with their candidacy for the job.

Step 6: Summarize Next Steps

Regardless of the impression the candidate has made, it is your responsibility to ensure the candidate feels as though they have been treated with respect and dignity during the interview and leaves with a positive impression of you and your company. Close the interview by thanking the candidate for their time and interest and advising them of the next steps in your selection process.

You may also want to provide a realistic time frame in which they may hear back and from whom or how. Saying something like *"We've had a lot of interest in this position and I have a few other candidates to consider. I should be making a decision within the next two weeks."* Be realistic and honest as they may have other opportunities to consider as well. Sometimes, if I know there was a better candidate, I may include *"If for some reason you don't hear before that we may have decided on another candidate."* Then follow up with a written communication to that effect so they can move on to other prospective companies and limit their wanting to call you for a status update. If you are interested in the applicant, do not tell the candidate that references will be checked or anything like that, because if references come back poorly, they may want to know what happened. Rather, indicate *"we will continue processing your application for employment"* then follow your internal process for next steps.

Never imply a candidate will be hired if you are unsure. An anxious candidate can interpret an overly encouraging remark as an implied offer. Statements that might lead a candidate to believe they will be hired are things like: *"it's in the bag"*, *"you will do great here"*, *"you are going to love working here"*, *"I'll see you later"*.

Shortly after the interview is concluded and the candidate has left, while your impressions are fresh, complete all your notes to objectively evaluate all the information you have received. Summarizing notes of key points relating to the job requirements is essential especially if you have multiple candidates. Then attach the form to the application.

There may also be times when you know that this candidate is the perfect fit for your position, when this happens, you'll want to continue the pre-employment process immediately if your organization has procedures in place to do so. Don't let the perfect candidate walk out of the door only to find another potential opportunity with another company. Time is of the essence to ensure you capture the most qualified individuals for the position.

P.R.I.D.E.S. Interview Model®

PREPARE
- Review their application or resume.
- Prepare Standard Interview Questions.
- Turn phones and computer sounds OFF.
- Know & Review job description and required KSA's.
- Know job specifics, hours, pay scale, schedule, etc.

RAPPORT BUILDING
- Sincerely welcome the candidate; create a casual rapport building environment by asking neutral open-ended questions or simply, *"How was your trip here?"*
- Be natural and relaxed, but remain professional.
- Show interest in the candidate as a person.
- Do not rush or make candidate feel hurried.
- Provide a comfortable setting and ensure privacy.

INFORMATION GATHERING
- To put the candidate at ease, advise you will be taking notes to remember key information.
- Ask similar questions of each candidate.
- Ask broad based, open-ended and behavior based questions depending on required KSA's.
- Ask follow-up questions as needed.
- Re-direct conversation when necessary.

DESCRIBE & DISCUSS
- Discuss Company Culture.
- Describe job specific responsibilities.
- Discuss hours, schedule, rate of pay, benefits etc.
- Describe general performance expectations.
- Whenever possible, provide a brief tour of the workplace. It's ok to let them experience the environment first hand.

EXPECT & ASK FOR QUESTIONS
- Ask the candidate if they have any questions.
- Thoroughly answer the candidates questions or get the information you may not know before they leave.
- Remember the candidate is making a decision whether to join the company too!

SUMMARIZE NEXT STEPS
- Thank the candidate for their time and interest.
- Tell them how, when and from whom they will hear in regards to the next steps in your hiring process such as, *"I have a few more interviews to conduct and anticipate a final decision"* and when.
- OR proceed with a conditional offer to hire.

The P.R.I.D.E.S. Model of Interviewing

After the P.R.I.D.E.S. Model of Interviewing™ is complete, as an interviewer, you are responsible for documenting the reasons you failed to hire an individual. You may also be responsible for communicating the decision to employ a candidate or not. When and if you do, you'll want to be sure the reasons are job related, valid and specific. General comments such as "no good" are insufficient and could leave your company open to criticism should a complaint be filed with a government agency. Some valid, more specific, factors in your candidate evaluation that might lead to declining to hire may include:

- Desires job for short period of time;
- Limited-service experience;
- Making excuses or placing blame;
- No smile or unfriendly attitude;
- Not asking questions/interacting with interviewer;
- Poor grooming or appearance;
- Speaking negatively about past employers;
- Unable to work the days and hours required;
- Unrealistic salary/wage expectation.

People are always wondering what to tell candidates who apply so I wanted to make a few suggestions. Obviously with the volume of candidates we want to discourage candidates from making status calls as much as possible, but it is bound to happen.

Here are some general suggestions depending on your situation:

Upon completing an application, candidates could be told: *"Applications and Resumes are reviewed by the appropriate managers and callbacks are made only to those candidates that we are interested in interviewing, if you will be interviewed, you could expect you to hear within a week or two"* Again, be realistic and honest as they may have other opportunities to consider as well.

If you are keeping good records and are using an applicant tracking system to capture candidate data, if a candidate calls after two weeks has passed, they might be told something like, *"Yes I see you applied on (date) and your number is (repeat their phone number) we have your application on file and they are reviewed by the appropriate hiring manager and callbacks are made only to candidates that managers are interested in interviewing"*. Telling the candidate when they applied and indicating the number on file reassures them that we know who they are. If you know the individual is not being considered for employment you should feel confident in saying something like, *"Yes I see you applied on (date) and your number is (repeat their phone number) I believe the manager has decided to consider other candidates at this time"*. If you are that hiring manager and haven't sent a written communication yet, then you should also feel confident to say, *"Yes, I see you applied/interviewed on (date) and your number is (repeat their phone number), while you did meet many of the qualifications, I've decided to consider other candidates at this time."* If, during any of these calls, you know the position they applied for has been filled, simply tell them, *"That position has been filled at this time."*

Rarely have I had a candidate ask why I chose one candidate over them. But it has happened, and in those moments, I provided the most honest developmental feedback possible. That person walks away knowing what they could have done differently to secure the position. Never make comments that compare that candidate to the one you hired, simply provide feedback that may be included in your notes from the conversation. So long as the reason is valid, job related and non-discriminatory, you should remain confident in the decision and your ability to advise that candidate.

If you are responsible for communicating the hiring decision, once you have completed any required pre-employment assessments, background checks and/or drug tests and they have been successfully completed, you can then contact the candidate and offer the position. Depending on your company, this offer process may be completed by the hiring manager, office manager, human resources representative or business owner. The offer is made and should include:

- The position being offered;
- The position status, full time, part time;

- Your preferred start date;
- A confirmation of the rate of pay;
- Their general work hours;
- Asking for their acceptance of the position.

Once they have formally accepted the position and you have a signed offer letter in hand, you can explain how your onboarding process works. This includes completing required federal state and/or locally regulated paperwork as part of your onboarding process. TheCompleteManagerMakeover.com website contains webinars and e-courses that provide the knowledge and skills required to manage the post-employment paperwork requirements.

Now that you have found the right person for the job, onboarding is a critical step to ensure all the time and effort put into finding them is not wasted because they leave the organization. Onboarding isn't just about the first 90 days; it can take more time when necessary. It starts the first day when The employee completes any new hire paperwork. It then proceeds to acclimate the employee to their specific position, policies and processes, layout of the office or location and then any of their specific job requirements. Often there are group orientations where new employees can meet one another whether in person or virtually. Onboarding also consists of providing opportunities to give and receive ongoing feedback within the first 30, 60 and 90 days of employment and beyond.

These steps in the onboarding process help to ensure that you reduce turnover. According to a recent gallup.com survey[4], *"The cost of Replacing an individual employee can range from one and a half to two times the employee's annual salary."* and *"Fifty-two percent of voluntarily exiting employees say their manager or organization could have done something to prevent them from leaving their job."*

---

[4] https://www.gallup.com/workplace/247391/fixable-problem-costs-businesses-trillion.aspx

This means we need to maximize a new hires success rate through proper Orientation and Onboarding among other things. It is important to note that orientation and onboarding are not the same. Orientation is about the meat and potatoes and getting somebody ready to work, like filling out paperwork, touring the workplace and the like. Onboarding is a lengthier process and much more comprehensive to ensure that the employee understands their role in the company, the organizational dynamics, and the culture as well. Onboarding and orientation go hand in hand to achieve the most successful retention possible.

When you see the statistics that 23% of employees leave within 6 months because they haven't received clear guidelines about their responsibilities[5], and 21% of employees leaving in the first six months said "more effective training" would have convinced them to stay[6], you know you need to establish clear onboarding processes. While new hire paperwork is an important first step, it is more important to ensure your employees are comfortable with their position, coworkers, company policy and surroundings. New Hire Onboarding should be developed to streamline your employee's ability to get quickly acclimated to the organization in all these ways. Most companies have HR technology systems where much of this process is now paperless. This paperwork also includes legally required documents as well as company policies that must be reviewed and acknowledged on day one of employment. New hire paperwork may include completing federal and state required forms, a review of key policies and procedures from an employee handbook, sharing personal information such as emergency contacts, discussing how and when an employee receives their schedule and paycheck. How often might we forget to explain where the restrooms are located and what the process and procedure is for lunch or break time? All of this and more should be reviewed with the employee. There is a Sample

---

5   www.shrm.org/hrdisciplines/staffingmanagement/articles/pages/onboarding-key-retaining-engaging-talent.aspx

6   www.shrm.org/hrdisciplines/staffingmanagement/articles/pages/onboarding-key-retaining-engaging-talent.aspx

Onboarding Checklist in The CMM Supplemental Workbook & Toolkit via download at https://thecompletemanagermakeover. com/thecmm/cmm-supplemental-toolkit/.

This checklist gives you lots of ideas and information regarding what should be discussed during the First day up to the first year of employment. It is the perfect way to make sure you don't forget anything when you are introducing the employee to the overall company. Sharing this information gives a new employee the guidelines and processes and procedures to reduce missteps during the first few months of employment. Taking the time to thoroughly review these details will show the new employee how important they are and how dedicated you are to their training and adjusting to the company.

Beginning with the new hire paperwork process and continuing with the new hire orientation checklist and beyond, the employee will go through specific job training. This training might be either one on one with key employees or a group orientation session if applicable. This will also introduce them to any other processes to further indoctrinate the employee to their job, the department, and the company overall. These steps are essential in the successful completion of their overall introduction.

While there are several strategies to ensure successful onboarding, one that is of great value is to assign a workplace P.A.L., which stands for Person Accelerating Learning, some workplaces call it a buddy. No matter what you call it, this individual can help an employee become acclimated to the rules, policies, procedures, social norms, and the workplace in general. The P.A.L. is someone who your organization deems well liked, highly skilled, and knowledgeable of the organizational dynamics and culture. Many companies designate their high performers for this type of initiative but you can also make it voluntary so employees can opt in if they want to. It's important to establish the length of time an employee will work with a new hire. Keep in mind that pairing new hires with pals from other departments can serve your organization well by improving cross departmental communication and synergies.

P.A.L.'s also provide support to the New employee by a establishing an individual with whom they can develop camaraderie. While the question might be controversial, Gallup's employee engagement surveys often ask, "Do you have a best friend at work?" The surveys consistently find that employees who have best friends at work lead to better performance.

Another excellent onboarding and retention best practice includes providing regular feedback to the employee. This feedback may include company expectations, the employees experiences and feedback regarding the employees performance during their first 90 days. These discussions can be documented through evaluations to give and get feedback on the employees first 30, 60 and 90 days. The right training and feedback provided to employees regarding their performance, both constructive or developmental is important to success and retaining good employees. Be sure to distribute a copy to all new hires regarding what is reviewed on the evaluations providing employees with more information about the expectations and helping to create more buy-in and commitment to objectives to be achieved during that onboarding period.

CHAPTER 3

FOUR STEPS TO EFFECTIVE TRAINING AND EVALUATING FOR SUCCESS

The dictionary defines training as the action of teaching a person a particular skill or type of behavior. In addition, the goal of training is to ensure your trainee retains as much information as possible in relation to the subject matter.

Ultimately, there are three roles in the training process, the trainee, the trainer or facilitator of training, and the advocate. The trainee, or the person learning is responsible to ensure a mind clear of distractions so that they can receive the information being disseminated. The trainee uses all available resources to drive their own performance and in the long term their knowledge base. Part of this includes taking advantage of all available resources when there are questions about what has been learned. Depending on the context of the training, the trainer's role is to use every method available to impart the learning to the trainee. We will discuss the various methods of training later in this chapter. The advocate's role in training is to support the training efforts. In some situations, human resource representatives conduct training or facilitates training while you, as a manager, are the supporter. But those roles might be reversed when you as the manager facilitate training and human resources or other internal colleagues become the supporter. The supporters' role is to ask employees questions regarding what they have learned and how they might be able to help them apply the new skills and concepts to the job. Supporters also take on the role of coach when employees are not effectively performing the skills or concepts they have learned.

It is important to understand why training is important in addition to reducing turnover and retaining good employees. When we retain good productive employees, it leads to reduced turnover thereby saving money by avoiding additional costly recruitment processes. It also strengthens the skills and abilities of your employees which in turn results in improved productivity for the organization. Training also helps improve underperforming areas, creates consistency of process within an organization and helps to improve morale.

For training to be effective we need to remember that adults learn differently than children. Adults typically have a world of experience they bring to the training and it is drawn on when encountering future experiences. This can hinder new learning as they seek to validate the new information based on their current beliefs and experiences. That validation will then dictate their choice to learn it or not. This can often be the reason for most questions that may come up during training, it is questioning the information against what they have experienced in the past. In addition, adults tend to decide for themselves whether something is important to be learned. Our adult minds also seek and expect that whatever we are learning will be immediately useful in some way. As we question the need for the new information, we want to understand what purpose the new learning will serve.

Because adults have past experiences that are brought to training, they may already have mixed views, so it is important to ensure adult learners are advised why the learning is important, what makes it different, why is it better. This way you can counteract the preconceived knowledge and viewpoints while encouraging a different way of thinking about the process. In addition, because adults bring these past experiences with them, it is important that you as the trainer, be open minded to discussion, questions, and opinions that may provide opportunities to improve or change the process. It is through this discussion, questioning and sharing of opinion that we actively participate in the training and promote a collaborative environment in which we function best.

In addition to learning differently, we also retain information at a higher rate based on the type of learning. In this model, the learning pyramid which is sometimes referred to as the Cone of Learning developed by the National Training Laboratory Institute of Applied Behavioral Science, suggests that some methods of study are more effective than others. This model is often applied to methods of training. There are seven levels of the pyramid and at the top of the pyramid we find Auditory. Auditory consists of simply hearing the information usually delivered in the form of a lecture or speech. According to the cone of learning this model suggests only 5% of the information is retained. As we move down the Cone of Learning two include visual and kinesthetic studying, we see the average retention rates increase. When we apply this model to training, we anticipate that the retention rate would equally increase. This model is important to training in that the trainer should use a combination of auditory visual and kinesthetic learning to maximize retention of the information.

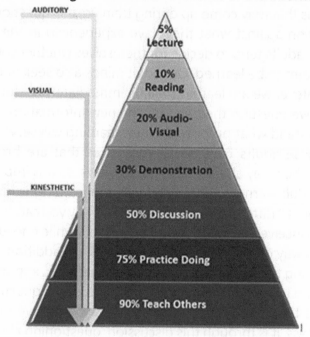

Adapted from the NTL Institute of Applied Behavioral Science Learning Pyramid

In adult learning, it is equally as important to understand that there are three aspects of effective face to face communication that include the words we speak, the tone and inflection in our voice and our nonverbal language known as body language. Understanding that each of these aspects can determine whether our communication during training is effective or ineffective.

- Are your words at a fast, moderate, or slow pace?
- Is your tone open and receptive or cold and condescending?
- What is happening with your nonverbal communication?
- What are your eyes and face doing?
- What are your arms doing?
- What is your posture communicating during training?

All these things are important to consider so that your trainee is open and receptive to the communications and training being conducted. No one wants to learn from someone using a condescending tone with their eyebrows ruffled. We have often heard it said that how we say what we say is important, but as we layer in the model of human behavior in a separate chapter, we will also see that who we say things to is equally as important.

Since everyone learns in a different way, using different techniques Is beneficial in making sure your trainee can maximize the learning. Let's take a closer look at the three Learning styles. This will help you tailor training toward an individual's learning style or by using a combination of all of them.

When they...	Visual	Auditory	Kinesthetic & Tactile
Spell	Do they try to see the word?	Do they sound out the word or use a phonetic approach?	Do they write the word down to find if it feels right?

When they...	Visual	Auditory	Kinesthetic & Tactile
Talk	Do they sparingly but dislike listening for too long? Do they favor words such as *see, picture,* and *imagine*?	Do they enjoy listening but are impatient to talk? Do they use words such as *hear, tune,* and *think*?	Do they gesture and use expressive movements? Do they use words such as *feel, touch,* and *hold*?
Concentrate	Do they become distracted by untidiness or movement?	Do they become distracted by sounds or noises?	Do they become distracted by activity around they?
Meet someone again	Do they forget names but remember faces or remember where they met?	Do they forget faces but remember names or remember what they talked about?	Do they remember best what they did together?
Contact people on business	Do they prefer direct, face-to-face, personal meetings?	Do they prefer the telephone?	Do they talk with them while walking or participating in an activity?
Read	Do they like descriptive scenes or pause to imagine the actions?	Do they enjoy dialog and conversation or hear the characters talk?	Do they prefer action stories or are not a keen reader?

When they...	Visual	Auditory	Kinesthetic & Tactile
Do something new at work	Do they like to see demonstrations, diagrams, slides, or posters?	Do they prefer verbal instructions or talking about it with someone else?	Do they prefer to jump right in and try it?
Put something together	Do they look at the directions and the picture?		Do they ignore the directions and figure it out as they go along?
Need help with a computer application	Do they seek out pictures or diagrams?	Do they call the help desk, ask a neighbor, or growl at the computer?	Do they keep trying to do it or try it on another computer?

Regardless of whether your trainee has a preference in learning, it is best to use a solid method of instruction. There are several methods of instruction and extensive research on training but I learned the Four Step Method of Training, Know, Show, Do, Review format early in my career and have always found it to be the most concise but also the best. If you ever had someone training you who didn't know all the right steps to the process, they may have begun showing you how to do something and then stopped to go back and start over. As a trainer you need to be sure that you know the exact process step by step, to avoid this error in training. You must know the whole process to break it down into manageable steps to teach. Here is some explanation of each of the steps:

Know the Process Thoroughly.

- Prepare for training.

- Break the whole process into parts.
- Lay out steps and key points.
- Outline exact sequence to prepare the learner.

Show the Learner the process.

- Explain the process as you demonstrate.
- <u>Describe</u> the process, step by step.
- Stress key points, <u>demonstrate </u>process step by step.

Do allow the learner to practice.

- Ask the learner to explain key points of the process.
- Direct the learner to complete a trial run of the process first.
- Correct along the way ensuring the learner performs process correctly.
- Ask questions to ensure understanding.

Review, follow-up and evaluate.

- Have the learner perform the process independently, refrain from taking control.
- Redirect processes as needed, intervene only when necessary.
- Check progress frequently, make corrections through positive coaching.

Know the Process Thoroughly.

- Prepare for training.
- Break the whole process into parts.
- Lay out steps and key points.
- Outline exact sequence to prepare the learner.

Show the Learner the process.

- Explain the process as you demonstrate.
- <u>Describe</u> the process, step by step.
- Stress key points, <u>demonstrate</u> process step by step.

Do allow the learner to practice.
- Ask the learner to explain key points of the process.
- Direct the learner to complete a trial run of the process first.
- Correct along the way ensuring the  learner performs process correctly.
- Ask questions to ensure understanding.

Review, follow-up and evaluate.
- Have learner perform process independently, refrain from taking control.
- Redirect processes as needed, intervene only when necessary.
- Check progress frequently, make corrections through positive coaching.

The Four Step Method of Training

CHAPTER 4

EVALUATIONS AND PERFORMANCE IMPROVEMENT CONVERSATIONS

Now that we have learned how to train our employees to maximize retention of the information, our next steps would be evaluating that performance. When we are conducting the training, we use the review step to ensure that we are making corrections through positive coaching. Then we must continuously ensure we provide feedback and evaluation of the continued use of that training.

As mentioned previously when discussing retention, providing feedback, and evaluating the first 30, 60 and 90 days of an employee's acclimation to employment and their progress is crucial. This sends the message that you care about the employee's performance and process, as well as them as a person. Typically, a 30/60/90 Day performance evaluation is the first evaluation given to employees. This must be done to ensure that along the introductory period you are communicating constructive feedback as well as addressing deficiencies to correct them prior to the end of the 90 days. To ensure a culture of collaboration I often provide a copy of the thirty 30/60/90-day evaluation form to all new hires. This helps the employee understand the clear upfront expectations in the first 90 days. A sample of a basic 30/60/90 Day performance evaluation can be found in The CMM Supplemental Workbook & Toolkit via download at https://thecompletemanagermakeover. com/thecmm/cmm-supplemental-toolkit/.

The performance evaluation process is important so that we can communicate positive feedback, recognize accomplishments, reward outstanding performance, correct deficiencies, redirect behavior, if necessary, communicate expectations and establish future goals. Performance evaluations may also be used as a basis for personnel decisions including such things as career development, salary increases, and corrective action, if appropriate. They also become a legal document which is why you must ensure you accurately reflect an employee's performance. The three main steps in the process are to prepare for the meeting, conduct the meeting, and then follow up.

In preparing for the performance evaluation discussion, you need to review what goals and objectives had been established previously ensure you seek the input from the employee and provide objective feedback. Just like the interview process can be affected by the Halo and Horns effect so too can the evaluation process so you want to be mindful of that as well.

Ratings Systems

There are various types of ratings systems used in performance evaluations. Your organization may or may not have one; however, I prefer a five-point rating scale. The five rating criteria include:

- Unsatisfactory
- Below Expectation
- Satisfactory/Average
- Above Average
- Outstanding

Establishing criteria for each of the ratings criteria will help support the most objective evaluations. Here is an example:

Outstanding: This category should be reserved for very select employees whose performance is rare.

- Far exceeds job standards
- Consistent peak performance even at most difficult tasks

- Extremely accurate
- Rarely makes errors
- Seizes initiative
- Exceptionally dependable
- Requires little direction and/or supervision

Above Average

- Better than standard
- Performance is consistently accurate
- Errors are few and seldom repeated
- Dependable follow-up
- Higher quality performance than most
- Better management skills than peers

Satisfactory/Average: As managers we are often reluctant to rate an employee as average however average indicates that the employee is doing exactly what they need to meet the standard but no more and no less. Most employees will perform at this level.

- Meets the standard
- Predictable performance with infrequent mistakes
- Finishes work on schedule
- Needs help on some assignments
- Satisfactory work quality and quantity
- Requires normal supervision
- "Competent" rating corresponds to a (3) on the performance evaluation

Below Expectation/Unsatisfactory: These ratings should rarely be used unless the employee is having performance issues and if an overall rating is a 2 outside of the probationary period an employee can be placed on probation due to performance.

- Unsatisfactory performance
- Inconsistently meets standards
- Requires more supervision and training than peers
- Cannot always be counted on

Just for fun I thought to include these humorous ratings scale I came across years ago adapted from the author and leadership consultant Bobb Biehl.

	Outstanding	Above Average	Average	Below Expectation	Unsatisfactory
Quality	Leaps tall buildings in a single bound	Must take a running start to leap over tall buildings	Can only leap over a short building with no spires	Crashes into building when attempting to jump over them	Cannot recognize buildings at all, not to mention jump
Timeliness	Is faster than a speeding bullet	Is as fast as a speeding bullet	Not quite as fast as a speeding bullet	Would you believe a slow bullet	Wounds self with bullet when attempting to shoot gun
Initiative	Is stronger than a locomotive	Is stronger than a bull elephant	Is stronger than a bull	Shoots the bull	Smells like a bull
Adaptability	Walks on water consistently	Walks on water in emergencies	Washes with water	Drinks water	Passes water in emergencies
Communication	Talks with God	Talks with angels	Talks to himself	Argues with himself	Loses those arguments

This chart may or may not be able to help with evaluations but it's important to know that there are some specific evaluator errors like the previously mentioned Halo and Horns effects.

Evaluator errors

- **Varying standards** – This happens when we are not consistent with the standards that we expect of each employee, while one employee is required to make 500 widgets in an hour another might be expected to make 400 in that timeframe. This is an example of varied standards.
- **Recency/primacy** – This effect is more common when discussing learning and has to do with the tendency that information presented in the beginning or end of a learning process is the only part that tends to be retained and the

information presented in the middle is not retained. This effect occurs when an evaluator has the tendency to only remember what happened recently or far in the past. Evaluators need to ensure that they are considering the entire evaluation period. Therefore, keeping a record of excellent performance or areas of opportunity is important. Doing so consistently throughout the employee's tenure provides a way to include information that encompasses the entire evaluation period.

- **Bias** – This occurs when we use race, color, religion, sex, national origin, disability age, veteran status, sexual orientation, political beliefs, or any other protected category as the basis for an evaluation rating. Not only does it create a subjective evaluation but it is also discriminatory and illegal.
- **Evaluation patterns** – This error occurs when the evaluator has the tendency to rate most people the same, always too moderate, or always too strict.
- **Contrast error** – A contrast error occurs when you compare one employee with another. You complete an evaluation for employee #1 and they had high ratings due to their truly outstanding performance. We then compare employee #2 using employee #1 as the benchmark or criteria. It is important that you evaluate everyone with the same ratings scale criteria but also based on the same established expectations criteria.

The ratings portion of evaluation should only be a part of it, establishing goals should be another. The use of a SMART[7] Goal is highly recommended because growth tends to occur more rapidly when we focus on setting specific goals. Goals should be developed by both the evaluating manager and the employee to be evaluated but can also be developed collaboratively to determine the final goals. These goals should be agreed upon for the review period. The words in the acronym have changed from time to time but below is a model that is often used.

---

[7]   SMART is an acronym that has been credited to both Peter Drucker (1955) and George. T. Doran (1991)

- **S**pecific – Objectives are detailed and focused. Action verbs such as evaluate, complete, develop, define, identify, learn, provide, and maintain, are often used.
- **M**easurable – Objectives must be quantifiable so that it is clear when it has been reached. Cost (reduce expenditures by x dollars), time (shorten process time by x hours), quantity (serve x more clients per day), quality (decrease customer complaints from x to y), and percentage of time (increase child car restraint usage by x%).
- **A**chievable – Objectives can be a "stretch," but must be attainable and realistic. They should not be too easy or too hard. Within the employee's control or influence.
- **R**esults-focused – Achievement of objectives is measured by outcomes (not activities) such as products, deliverables, and accomplishments. The outcome is a result of activities. Objectives should be relevant to the mission and overall organizations goals.
- **T**ime-focused – Achievement of objectives has a specific deadline and it is clear when has been accomplished. A target date is defined.

I often suggest the use of the smart objectives in conjunction with a specific rating on the ratings scale. For example, you could outline the objective in the SMART format stating, *Increase overall revenue by 10% before September 30th, 2021,* and it contains all the criteria for a SMART objective. But you can take it one step further and include the rating an employee will receive for not only attainment of the goal, but also what rating will be assigned should they under or over perform. It could be outlined stating *Increase overall revenue by 8%-10% before September 30th, 2021, with ratings assigned as follows:*

> *Outstanding = above 15% Increase*
> *Above Average = 10% – 15 % Increase*
> *Average = 8% - 10% Increase*
> *Below Expectation = 5% - 8% Increase*
> *Unsatisfactory = Under 5% Increase*

Once the evaluation is completed with objective ratings and established goals you will need to prepare for the meeting. Involving the employee in preparing for the meeting includes agreeing on a time and place to conduct the evaluation and asking the employee for a self-evaluation in advance. This helps to identify any differences in how the employee and the manager view performance. Having this in advance helps to prepare discussion points to address these differences.

When conducting the performance evaluation conversation, it is important to put the employee at ease first. During the conversation you should be objective, honest and candid. Keep focused and rate the work results not the individual person. Try not to talk too much and when the employees nonverbal cues dictate, ask the employee for their opinion or feedback.

When you go into the conversation, review the ratings for each of the respective categories one by one, discussing examples, highlighting strengths or areas of opportunity as you go. Be sure to listen to the employee's point of view as well as how they rated themselves and why, especially when it is inconsistent with your own rating. There should be no surprises when reviewing performance ratings and standards so long as you have made certain to address performance issues both good and developmental as things occurred throughout the evaluation period. Once you cover the ratings section of the evaluation you can then discuss and agree on mutual objectives for the coming evaluation period. Once you have completed reviewing the evaluation ratings and the objectives, you should ask for their signature and written feedback. It is particularly important to do so, as to get the employee to acknowledge, in writing, that the conversation occurred. Some employees choose to provide the comments right away while others may want to take a day or two. I recommend you close the loop on the evaluation and performance process no later than the next day. Finally, be sure to provide the employee with a copy of the review as this can provide a written record of the highlights of the discussion and a way for them to recall the mutually agreed upon objectives.

On occasion you may encounter a situation where your ratings and the employee's ratings are vastly different. This may occur because ongoing feedback of both good performance and opportunities of improvement are not addressed throughout the evaluation period. An employee should always know how they are doing because a good manager provides consistent effective feedback. Nonetheless there will be times when you will have differing opinions of the performance. In those situations, encourage the employee to attach a written response to the review so that their point of view is included as part of the document.

Once the performance evaluation is completed it is important that you regularly follow up to provide ongoing feedback and coaching to reinforce learning, correct deficiencies, teach new skills and modify goals as needed, being sure to keep records for use during the next evaluation discussion.

Correcting Performance Issues

To be effective, corrective action should correct or improve the behavior of the employee who is not meeting proper standards of conduct or performance. Gradual levels of corrective action can be invoked to allow the manager to administer the appropriate level of corrective action consistent with the infraction. This gradual corrective action process should increase the individual's effectiveness. There is a common view that "discipline" always means punishment. In my opinion it is quite possibly because the dictionary's definition of discipline is "the practice of training people to obey rules or a code of behavior using punishment to correct disobedience". It's no wonder that "discipline" when used in the workplace is not viewed positively. Punishment should be the last resort of an effective manager in achieving corrective action. Punishment rarely motivates the employee; it will more than likely result in the minimum response necessary to avoid further punishment. Corrective Action is a more appropriate term because that it what these performance conversations set out to accomplish.

Performance infractions can range from minor to major issues which will dictate the level of corrective action. A one-time lateness may not rise to the level of a written notice when a coaching conversation is sufficient to address the incident. Let's look at various types of infractions.

Levels of Infractions

Typically, there are three levels of infractions. Minor, intermediate, and Major. In some situations, a minor infraction could be considered a major one based on the circumstance. For example: failure to attend a scheduled meeting may be typically considered a minor infraction but when it is a mandatory meeting it may rise to the level of an intermediate or major infraction.

Examples of Minor Infractions may include:

- Failure to attend scheduled meetings.
- Loitering and loafing during working hours.
- Leaving the assigned working areas during working hours without permission.
- Failure to be at the workstation at starting time.
- Creating or contributing to unsanitary conditions.
- Neglect or mishandling of equipment or any other supplies.
- Unsatisfactory work and/or attitude

Examples of Intermediate Infractions may include:

- Leaving the premises during working hours without permission of a supervisor.
- Two days unexcused absence during any thirty calendar days or equivalent policy/practice.
- Violation of a "no solicitation/no distribution" rule.
- Failure to report off from work in accordance with current policy.
- Failure to comply with Company Standards.

Examples of Major Infractions may include:

- Deliberately making or using falsified records, material requisitions, timecards.
- Violence in Workplace - Attempting bodily injury to another.
- Insubordination.
- Theft of property.
- Reporting for work under the influence of any alcoholic beverage or illegal narcotics.
- Willful/careless destruction of company property.
- Violation of safety rules.
- Sleeping on duty.
- Possession of firearm or other illegal weapon on company premises.

Before resorting to written corrective action, it is important that you take appropriate measures such as the following:

- Determine whether there is support for the action. Are there witnesses? What proof exists that the employee made a policy infraction?
- Collect any proof or meet with witnesses before taking corrective action.
- Obtain the actual physical evidence and information essential to the infraction before taking corrective action; e.g., copies of sick leave record, timecard record for lateness etc.
- Review in as much detail as possible the information you already have regarding the employee.
- Tell the employee why you are taking corrective action; be as specific as possible.
- Has the employee received prior corrective action notices? Are you sure the employee understood this notice?
- Has the employee had sufficient time to correct the problem?
- Have you taken all possible steps to correct the behavior?

- Is corrective action consistent with the past practice?
- Did you consider the employee's point of view?
- Have you considered personal difficulties or mitigating circumstances?
- Corrective Action should not be a surprise.
- Have you reviewed your actions with another objective manager, such as supervisors or Human Resources personnel.

Corrective Action Steps

Organizations typically have a few steps in their corrective action process and any violation of policies and procedures is misconduct and appropriate for corrective action procedures in most cases. For corrective action to be viewed as fair, the corrective action step should fit the violation. Examples of corrective action include, but may not be limited to:

1. ***Coaching and Counseling:*** Effective coaching and counseling sessions raise employees' awareness of poor performance or disruptive behaviors and provide specific positive recommendations for solution. These sessions are verbal in nature and generally occur primarily to inspire and support the employee for long-term development.

2. ***Verbal notice:*** This is given at the first offense of a minor offense or at the first sign of poor performance. It includes a problem-solving discussion, allowing both the manager and the employee to address concerns and encourages self-correction. Although the notice is verbal, written documentation should be made and it must be signed by the employee and placed in the employee file. A verbal notice is a formal communication notifying an employee of the actual beginning of the disciplinary process. The verbal notice should be clearly announced to the employee. It is not acceptable to have a casual conversation concerning performance and later claim this

served as the verbal notice. Some organizations use a dual verbal notice policy-the first without a witness; the second with a witness present. While the content of the conversation may vary a general discussion consists of some or all these steps.

- Formal acknowledgement that the meeting constitutes a verbal/written notice. "This discussion is a verbal/ written notice and formally begins our progressive corrective action process. It is my hope that further corrective action steps will not be necessary."
- Clear identification and documentation of the poor performance or disruptive behavior. "The performance has not been acceptable and here is why..." or "The disruptive behavior continues despite our previous discussion. Here are some specific examples..."
- Restatement of the standards, objectives, and expectations of the organization. "The expectations are ..." (Substantiated by whatever legitimate documentation is available, that is, policy manuals, signed agreements.)
- State the specific correction necessary. General statements are *not* acceptable. The correction must be specific and measurable. "Here is what is necessary to improve the performance and avoid future disciplinary measure..." This is a perfect opportunity to reiterate the policy or procedure.
- Statement of how ongoing performance will be measured. (The employee must have reasonable access to the measurement.) "Your improved performance will be measured by..."
- Specific timeline for performance and behavior correction. "Your performance must meet our minimum standards of ___ within ___ days."
- Statement of ongoing monitoring tools and methods of feedback on performance. "We will meet again in two weeks to discuss progress."

- What is an appropriate timeline? The length of the timeline is determined by the process involved as well as past policy. employees must be given enough time to correct their performance. If it will take a month to turn the performance around, you cannot give them only two weeks to do so. If you give employees six months to correct their performance, you are sending the message that their poor performance is not a critical issue. If you can wait six months for employees to correct their problems, *you do not have a problem!* Only fix things that really matter. Thirty-day timelines or increments are most appropriate. However, all factors must be considered.

- Statement of managerial support to help the employee make the correction. "Our goal is to correct these performance deficiencies and avoid any further action. Here is what I/we will do to assist you."

- Identify additional resources available. "Copies of our training manuals will be available." "You may attend another training class or seminar." "Our trainer will spend ____ days with you in the next ____ weeks to provide additional training."

- Restatement/summary of the verbal notice. It is extremely important to test the effectiveness of the verbal notice communication. Have employees summarize and repeat back in detail their understanding of the notice. It is important to determine what information got through. It is the manager's job to determine employees' level of comprehension. If they do not understand their responsibility for correction, or the consequences of not doing so, the chance of successful change is slim.

Never threaten to fire the employee. Such threats are based on emotions, punishment, and retribution and are not traits of a respected or effective leader.

At the time of the verbal notice, a written summary of the meeting should be created and given to the employee. A copy should be placed in documentation files. Depending on your policy, this does not constitute a formal written notice. It serves as a formal recap of the verbal notice/ conversation and is a part of your ongoing documentation. Failure to correct the poor performance after verbal notice results in escalating the process to the next level.

3. ***Written notice:*** This may follow a verbal notice or serve as a first action based on the seriousness of the offense or poor performance. This step advises the employee that behavior or performance is unacceptable and requires immediate correction. This type of corrective action requires extensive documentation of the incident or situation, a discussion with the employee, and any comments the employee may want to include. The written notice is an escalation step in the disciplinary process. It indicates a continued lack of success in addressing the problem, along with an increase in the seriousness of the situation. This is also the first official notification of the existence of a significant performance or behavior problem.

The written notice is primarily the verbal notice put in writing, with a copy being placed as permanent record in the employee's personnel file. It follows the same format as the verbal notice with the following additions:

- The written notice begins with a summarization of the previous counseling sessions and verbal notices (frequency, dates, times).
- The consequence of the written notice is obviously different. It must be clearly identified (either a second written notice or form of suspension in compliance with your existing policy).

At the completion of the written notice session, the employee is asked to sign the document and is given a copy. The employee may refuse to sign the document but don't be distracted by any negative behavior. It might be helpful to indicate that their signature does not indicate that they agree with the documentation it simply indicates that the document was reviewed with them. If the employee still refuses to sign you can simply provide an opportunity for the employee to include their own comments. The employee's signature is not necessary but at this point a witness should be included in the conversation. The witness, truthfully and accurately, corroborates that the employee was asked to sign, refused to do so, and was given a complete copy of the document.

If a second written notice is appropriate, follow this same format, including the first written notice information in the opening summary and address the next step consequence. If the written notice does not result in appropriate performance or behavior change, the process may escalate to suspension or termination.

4. **Suspension:** Typically, a step in corrective action for a serious violation of rules or policies where an employee demonstrated repeated clear disregard for policies and rules. While some organizations use this as a step of corrective action it is recommended that this step of corrective action be used to review the employees overall performance history and decide if the employee should be terminated based on that history and considering the infraction that caused the suspension. suspension should typically last three days which allows time to investigate any circumstances that lead to the suspension and review the employee's full performance history to determine if employment will be separated. suspension impresses upon employees the seriousness of their circumstance,

provides a period of reflection and possibly time to realize the potential outcomes while the final decision is made. Whenever possible, discussing the overall decision with executive leaders tasked with decisions to hire, correct performance, and terminate is essential as it provides another opportunity to ensure all progressive corrective action, if any, to date is accurate and thorough enough to warrant separation of the employees employment. The documentation of the suspension including date of suspension and scheduled time to return for the determined outcome should be completed on an employee corrective action notice and signed by the employee AT THE TIME OF SUSPENSION. This ensures that you clearly communicate the date and time to return for the outcome of the decision. If date/time must be modified (typically only due to the need for additional investigatory time) contact the employee immediately to modify the date and time making note on the original corrective action form.

5. ***Returning from suspension:*** Typically when an employee returns from a suspension, there are a few possible outcomes: 2) there are mitigating circumstances causing the return of the employee to work and the employee must correct the performance/behavior, 2) the employee chooses to resign, 3) employment is terminated. If the employee is returned to work and desires to improve performance, encouragingly and positively welcome them back. Compile a written document that summarizes the steps in the disciplinary process to date and if appropriate, indicate that further infractions may result in dismissal. Ask the employee to sign this document and give them a copy. At this stage rarely will an employee refuse to be cooperative or to sign the document. The employee realizes the seriousness of the situation and usually demonstrates positive cooperation and compliance. If the employee resigns upon return from the suspension, process the resignation immediately and issue the final check based on your state's regulations. It is possible that an employee may offer to work

out a notice but you are under no obligation to accept it. One of the worst things you can do is to allow a previously suspended employee to work out a resignation notice. Sometimes sabotage, worker's compensation claims, theft, destruction of records, or a continued general undermining of management can result. An employee set on extracting retribution can do a lot of damage.

When the employee signs the documentation and returns to work, one of two things will happen:

- The employee successfully corrects his/her behavior or performance, and everyone lives happily ever after. This success story will add to your reputation as a highly skilled manager, capable of eliciting turnaround performance.
- The employee fails to live up to the agreement and the unacceptable behavior or poor performance continues. If this happens, the employee must be dismissed. Failure to do so destroys the credibility of the organization and the entire disciplinary process. If the employee is not dismissed, it proves not only to this employee, but to all others as well, that you are not willing to enforce company standards and expectations, these policies are not to be taken seriously, and you are unwilling to act.

6. ***Separation from employment***: This is the most severe form of corrective action administered. This action should be invoked when all other forms of problem-solving efforts have failed or when the seriousness of the offense warrants permanent removal of the individual from the workplace. This step usually takes place after a careful investigation has been conducted and sufficient prior corrective efforts have been taken and documented in the employee file. These corrective efforts should demonstrate the employer's efforts to increase the value

of the employee to the organization and demonstrate the employee's disregard for compliance with the employer's rules and/or policies. A Termination Guide and Discussion Checklist is available to provide detailed insight regarding the Termination Discussion and can be found here: https://thecompletemanagermakeover.com/product/e-book-guide-to-conducting-a-respectable-termination-session/

A Corrective Action Checklist that outlines what you should do at each point of the corrective action process is available in the Appendix.

REMEMBER: A successful corrective action conversation keeps the following in mind:

- Hold it in a private place so conversations cannot be overheard.
- Do not have a third-party present (unless acting as a witness)
- Take steps ahead of time to ensure no interruptions telephone calls, etc.
- Do not discuss in public places such as coffee houses or restaurants due to too many distractions to be successful.
- Do not start coaching session until you are in control of emotions.
- Have specific description of behavior to be discussed, i.e.: specific incidents of lateness, amount of time late as related to scheduled work time.
- Be prepared to substantiate the importance of desired performance as well as non-performance.
- Decide ahead what possible alternative solutions are and when you expect performance to improve.

After the initial conversation it is critical to follow up as well as celebrate improved performance.

Once you have determined the corrective action step to take and the level of infraction, you need to complete a corrective action document to provide a record of the conversation. Some organizations may already have a form for this purpose but if not, here are some tips and necessary details that should be included in the corrective action documentation depending on the situation.

1. Name: Ensure Legibility and accuracy of spelling
2. Department/Position
3. Date of Incident: Enter Date infraction Occurred (time if appropriate)
4. Date of Notice: Enter the date when the Notice is Given (not the day you intended to issue it)
5. This should be within 48hrs whenever possible (exceptions may include extra time for investigation, unable to issue due to the employee not working scheduled to work)
6. Category of infraction, if necessary (Policy, Attendance, Safety)
7. Details and Corrective Action. Be Specific and detail:
   a. Who was involved?
   b. What happened?
   c. Where did it happen?
   d. When did it happen, include exact times and dates, etc.
   e. Do you have proof (punch detail, schedule, charge receipt, video clip, photograph)?
   f. Explain what needs to be done to correct the behavior.

8. Action Taken: Indicate what level of counseling was applied to the infraction (Verbal, Written)
9. suspension Date if suspended.
10. Return Date: Enter date and time employee is to return to HR for employment decision if Suspension was conducted.
11. Previous Discipline history: If it's not documented it didn't happen.
12. Signatures: Manager Issuing Documentation or Witness when required.
13. Employee Comments and Signature: Have the employee write their own comments, sign, and date.

This checklist will help you prepare for a Performance Improvement Discussion.

Performance Improvement Conversations Checklist

CHAPTER 5

LOOKING AT THE LEGALITIES

There were several pivotal events in my career where in my position as the HR director or senior human resources designee where I had to communicate in some very tough situations. Throughout the years I had to correct employee performance through documentation, conduct termination conversations, and manage conversations with senior leaders. As I moved up the "ranks" I also had to deal with various types of conflict in the workplace, and that was just the beginning.

One of the toughest situations in my leadership journey would come when I was still a young human resources executive. At the age of 32 I became the Director of Human Resources at the famed Fontainebleau Hotel on Miami Beach. This was a massive hotel, it was Miami Beach's most renowned landmark hotel, situated during 20 lush tropical acres overlooking the Atlantic Ocean. It was comprised of three buildings with 1195 rooms and suites, 26 departments and over 1100 employees. It was a coveted position in the hospitality industry and one that I was excited and honored to have been hired to assume.

How could I have known that I would be at this stage in my career when the 9-11 attacks[8] took place. That morning began like any other morning as I prepared to go to work unaware of what the day would bring, not to mention the weeks and months ahead. It was around 9:15 in the morning when a buzz began throughout the office and hallways just outside the HR Department. The Director of Security came in my offices to tell me we needed to go to the employee entrance to watch TV. As we stood in the employee entrance watching the TV, we couldn't help but look at the television, then simultaneously, as if in slow motion, we turned towards each other with the realization of what we'd just been watching. We saw one of the Twin Towers on fire and within moments we saw an object, clearly resembling a plane, crash into the second Tower. As a native New Yorker this vision struck a chord for me in so many ways. We watched in horror as the newscaster explained what they believed was happening. Was it an accident in flight plans or was it more than that? It was a terrorist attack. It wouldn't be long before the executive team banded together to discuss what the next steps, outcome strategy, and probable fall out of this major event. Within days we were communicating with employees who had loved ones who lived in New York to ascertain their personal impact and put them in touch with our EAP and provide whatever support we could. Weeks turned into months and the travel and hospitality industries braced for impact. Revenues were decreasing more and more due to lack of US and International travel. Within a year of the 911 Attack, I would be responsible for coordinating the mass layoff of over 200 employees. This event would also trigger the WARN

---

[8] (From History.com https://www.history.com/topics/21st-century/9-11-attacks) On September 11, 2001, 19 militants associated with the Islamic extremist group al Qaeda hijacked four airplanes and carried out suicide attacks against targets in the United States. Two of the planes were flown into the twin towers of the World Trade Center in New York City, a third plane hit the Pentagon just outside Washington, D.C., and the fourth plane crashed in a field in Shanksville, Pennsylvania. Almost 3,000 people were killed during the 9/11 terrorist attacks.

Act[9], an employment law requiring the hotel to notify employees in advance regarding the impending layoff. In preparation, I developed a communication plan, and an organizational strategy. With the support of my HR team, we developed a communication tool for every employee that outlined everything they needed to know about the layoff. Those major layoffs at the Fontainebleau would be one of saddest times in my career. I can only hope that the compassion to serve those affected through the coordinated effort to empathetically communicate all the information, resources and support available for every employee made that difficult time just a bit easier to bear. Each individual effected was given personalized information including other job opportunities in the area, information about how to apply for the various re-employment services, documentation regarding how to apply for the extension of their medical benefits or government services for which they might be eligible, etc. The conversation took at least 35-45 minutes per employee. I conducted a training session with the Executive Committee to train them about the conversation, the contents of the binder and the expectation that these conversations be conducted with compassion, kindness and concern for every person affected. Somehow the Department of Labor got wind of what we were doing and to my surprise they requested a copy of our lay off binder. It was their intention to share it with other employers who were experiencing similar circumstances and who could benefit from our example to handle and manage the process in a humanitarian way. That call, among so many other things in my career, was further realization and confirmation that while the responsibility of managing people especially on such a large scale is a huge responsibility, the tough conversations can always be had while "ensuring that employees walk out of their manager's office with their dignity intact".

---

[9]   From dol.gov https://www.dol.gov/agencies/eta/layoffs/warn) The Worker Adjustment and Retraining Notification (WARN) Act helps ensure advance notice in cases of qualified plant closings and mass layoffs.

In fact, during one day of conversations (they lasted 3 days in total) I was conducting the conversation with one gentleman, who I will never forget, I'll call him Joe. We'd always had a friendly relationship in the workplace, we'd interact often, and he was in the purchasing department. As I finished up the conversation, asking again if he had any questions, he looked at the binder of information, looked back at me, then again at the binder and sat back in his chair. I had no idea what to expect, after all, the bottom line is that I'd just told him he was no longer employed. As he sat back in his chair staring at me and the binder he asked, "Miss Lisa, are you having this conversation with everyone?". In the back of my mind, I knew while there was no way I could have this conversation with all 200 plus individuals affected, I had trained all the executive team that would be having the conversations with their employees in the same manner, hoping that they were having the conversations with the compassion and sensitivity I had expected. I looked back at Joe and answered, "Well it's impossible for me alone to have these conversations but I'm having these conversations with many of those affected, but to answer your question, yes, other executives are having conversations such as this with their affected employees, everyone is getting this information to support them going forward." Baffled and a little confused and taken aback he said, in the most heartfelt sincere way I'd ever heard him speak, "Thank you", he said. His words shook me to my core and to this day as I write these words nothing has made my work as a manager and especially as a human resources manager more rewarding than that moment with those two words. As I write that story, I remember Joe and have often searched for him. I can't help but still choke up at that moment it my career. There will always be times when you must have a tough conversation, whether it's trying to improve someone's performance, trying to understand why they're not achieving or accomplishing their goals, or any number of issues. Termination discussions whether caused by the employee or uncontrollable layoff conversations are not easy for either person, but they can be had with compassion and empathy. All those discussions must be handled legally, with civility and respect by simply putting yourself in that person's shoes, even if for that moment.

I share that story because it required the hotel to look at several employment laws that would regulate that situation. Managing people, whether you are in human resources or not, requires you, as a manager, to know enough about the various employment law regulations to ensure compliance. If you do not know enough about the employment law to ensure your actions are in compliance or when to reach out to someone who does, (so they can get involved), you run the risk of getting yourself and your company in serious legal trouble. This chapter will highlight or detail some of the most important federal regulations that you, as a manager, should be aware of so that you can reach out to your leadership or your human resources representative should you encounter a situation that requires further insight and potentially their support to maintain compliance.

Fair Labor Standards Act (FLSA) (1938)_FLSA is an all-encompassing federal law that regulates minimum wage, overtime, equal pay, child labor, worker independent contractor status among other things. Although you may not be personally responsible for administering the provisions of FLSA, you need to understand some of its basic requirements and how they affect you and your employees.

The first thing you need to know about FLSA is that its provisions apply only to some employees. Nonexempt employees are covered by FLSA's minimum wage and overtime provisions. Nonexempt employees are usually those who are paid on an hourly basis and eligible for overtime pay. Exempt employees are not covered by the overtime provisions of FLSA. Exemption status is based on specific criteria including job duties, responsibilities educational qualifications, supervision duties and a federally established minimum salary. Designating an employee as exempt requires careful review to ensure compliance with the FLSA. Just because you give an employee the title "Manager" does not make them automatically exempt from overtime.

The Federal FLSA minimum wage requirements can be superseded by state laws that are more favorable to employees. Therefore, when a state's minimum wage is higher than the established federal minimum wage, employers are obligated to pay the higher rate. In addition, you must post notices outlining federal minimum wage and overtime requirements in prominent places so that employees can see them as they enter and leave the workplace. You can obtain posters at no cost from the U.S. Department of Labor, Wage and Hour Division.

The FLSA requires employers to pay minimum wage for all hours an employee works and overtime for all hours worked over 40 hours in each workweek. Overtime requires employers to pay 1½ times a nonexempt employee's regular rate of pay for any hours worked more than 40 hours in each workweek. Hours worked by an employee include all the time an employee must be on duty or on the work premises or at any other prescribed place of work, as well as any additional time the employee is permitted to work. The criteria for hours work may include travel time, changing time, waiting time, training time and doesn't stop there so you'll need to educate yourself. For the purposes of FLSA, the workweek is a period of 168 hours during seven consecutive 24-hour periods. A workweek doesn't have to correspond to a calendar week. It may begin on any day of the week and at any hour of the day.

Recording work time is an important issue since it impacts on overtime and pay issues. While time clocks are not required under FLSA, they are the most efficient and accurate way to record work hours of nonexempt employees. Any effective means for tracking hours may be used. You should not fail to count any part, however small, of an employee's regular work time and ensure employees are completely relieved of work duties during meal breaks otherwise it may be considered work time that must be paid.

FLSA also requires equal pay for equal work, and this requirement applies to all employees, exempt and nonexempt. Employers must ensure that male and female employees are paid equal wages for performing substantially equal jobs under the federal Equal Pay Act. If two jobs require equal skill, effort, and responsibility, and are performed under similar working conditions, they are considered equal for the purposes of determining wages.

Pay differentials based primarily on gender are prohibited by the Equal Pay Act of 1963. Minor differences in the degree of skill required or in job responsibilities cannot be used to justify a pay differential between male and female employees. Pay differentials within a job classification, however, are permitted if they are justified by: (1) a merit system, (2) a seniority system, (3) a system based on quality or quantity of production, or (4) any factor other than gender. Factors other than gender could include jobs in the same classification performed in different physical locations or under substantially different working conditions.

As previously mentioned, the FLSA regulates Independent contractors who are also exempt from minimum wage and overtime requirements. Although there is no true definition of an independent contractor, they are generally considered to be workers who contract with the company to provide specialized or requested services on a project or as-needed basis. The IRS has developed guidelines to help decide whether a worker can or should be classified as an independent contractor. These guidelines, known as the reasonable basis test, can be useful for FLSA purposes as well. Although others in the organization may be the ones to apply the guidelines, you should nevertheless understand how the decisions are made.

Child labor laws are also part of the Fair Labor Standards Act. Their purpose is to protect children from working in dangerous occupations, for excessive hours, and at unsuitable times of day or night. Child labor laws apply to all employees under the age of 18 and managers should consider both Federal and State regulations when seeking guidance for compliance. Much like the minimum wage, the regulation with the highest threshold should be applied.

Immigration Reform & Control Act (IRCA) (1986) Requires that new employees provide specific documents to employers showing that they are who they claim to be and that they have a legal right to work in the United States. These documents are detailed on a Federal Form I-9, which is typically completed during new hire paperwork with the human resources representative. It is important for managers to know that employees can provide any of the listed documents on Form I-9 and you should not make specific requests such as telling the prospective employee to, "bring in your driver's license and social security card" as this practice could be considered discriminatory. Every employee is required by law to complete the form no later than the 1st day of employment, it is illegal for employers and their managers to schedule employees to work prior to the completion of this Federally required documentation.

Occupational Safety & Health Act (OSHA) (1970) Mandates compliance with federal health & safety standards. The following are select OSHA requirements that apply to many general industry employers.

Hazard Communication Standard. This standard is designed to ensure that employers and employees know about hazardous chemicals in the workplace and how to protect themselves. Employers with employees who may be exposed to hazardous chemicals in the workplace must prepare and implement a written Hazard Communication Program and comply with other requirements of the standard.

Emergency Action Plan Standard. OSHA recommends that all employers have an Emergency Action Plan. An Emergency Action Plan describes the actions employees should take to ensure their safety in a fire or other emergency.

Fire Safety. OSHA recommends that all employers have a Fire Prevention Plan.

Exit Routes. All employers must comply with OSHA's requirements for exit routes in the workplace.

Walking/Working Surfaces. Ensures safety of all Floors, aisles, platforms, ladders, stairways, and other walking/working surfaces that are present. Slips, trips, and falls from these surfaces constitute most general industry accidents.

Medical and First Aid. OSHA requires employers to provide medical and first-aid personnel and supplies commensurate with the hazards of the workplace.

Depending on the industry, additional Safety Standards may include Machine Guarding (e.g., saws, slicers, shears, slitters, power presses, etc.), Lockout/Tagout for securing machinery, Electrical Hazards, Personal Protective Equipment (PPE), Respirators, Excessive Noise (E.G., Conditions That Make Normal Conversation Difficult), Confined Spaces, Blood Or Bodily Fluids, Powered Industrial Trucks

Health Insurance Portability and Accountability Act (HIPAA) Provides protections for participants and beneficiaries in group health plans, including limiting exclusions for preexisting medical and general health conditions. It also establishes privacy protections for employees against unauthorized disclosure of health-related information. As a manager you'll want to ensure you don't discuss or let other employees discuss an employee's personal and private health matters, illnesses, injuries etc., with anyone except those who need to know about it like your human resources representative or executive leader who manages these types of situations.

Uniformed Services Employment & Reemployment Rights Act (1994) Prohibits discrimination against military service members because of past, current, or future military service. Protects military service workers, employment rights and benefits of employment.

National Labor Relations Act (NLRA) (Wagner Act) (1935) Prohibits employers from certain unfair labor practices. Primary responsibility for enforcement rests on the National Labor Relations Board.

Labor-Management Relations Act (Taft-Hartley) (1947) Protects management rights by prohibiting certain unfair labor practices by unions.

Employee Retirement Income Security Act (ERISA) (if offer benefits) (1974) Establishes standards and requirements for the administration of employee benefit and welfare plans, to ensure employees will receive monies they set aside for a pension plan. The act also covers part-time employees working 1,000 hours a year.

Uniform Guidelines of employee Selection Procedures (1978) Prohibits selection policies and practices from having an adverse impact on the employment opportunities for any race, sex, or ethnic group unless it is a business necessity.

Federal Insurance Contributions Act (FICA) (1935) A federal payroll tax imposed on both employees and employers to fund Social Security and Medicare, which provides benefits to retirees, disabled, and children of deceased workers.

Worker Adjustment & Retraining Notification Act (WARN) (1989) Requires employers to give notice of plant closings or layoffs, such as in the case of the Fontainebleau story. This Act is triggered when the established formula is met based on the number of employees affected.

Title VII, Civil Rights Act (1964) (1991) Prohibits discrimination in all terms and conditions of employment (including pay and benefits) based on race, religion, ethnic group, sex, national origin, or disability. Areas of employment relationship that are included but may not be limited to: Hiring, Firing, Transfers, Evaluations, Assignments, Promotions, Compensation, Reduction in Workforce, Benefits, Training Programs etc.

Title I, Americans with Disabilities Act (1990) (ADA) Managers should refrain from asking questions such as medical problems, workers compensation history, absenteeism history, need for reasonable accommodation, nature, or severity of medical conditions.

Consolidated Omnibus Budget Reconciliation Act (COBRA) (1985) Employers with 20 or more employees are usually required to offer COBRA coverage and to notify their employees of the availability of such coverage. COBRA coverage allows employees and their qualified beneficiaries to remain covered under an employers Group health plan by opting to keep the coverage and pay for premiums. Employers must adhere to strict timeframes for notifying employees of their ability to take advantage of COBRA so managers should ensure they always notify their Human Resources representatives regarding employees who are no longer employed or whose hours are significantly reduced.

Age Discrimination in Employment Act (ADEA) (1967) Protects certain applicants and employees 40 years of age and older from discrimination based on age in hiring, promotion, discharge, compensation, or terms, conditions, or privileges of employment. Also prohibits mandatory retirement and/or age limits for jobs.

Family Medical Leave Act (FMLA) (1993) Provides that employees who have worked at least 12 months and at least 1,250 hours in the previous 12 months are eligible to take up to 12 weeks leave during any 12 month period for the purposes of: birth, adoption, or foster care of a child; caring for a spouse, child, or parent who has a serious health condition; or serious health condition of employee. This act is triggered whether an employee makes a request for this leave or not, so be sure to contact your HR representative when an employee is absent for two or more days due to illness, injury, or other serious health condition. Additionally, the National Defense Authorization Act of 2008 amends FMLA to allow a spouse, parent, son, daughter or next of kin up to 26 weeks to care for a member of the armed services suffering injuries or illness sustained while on active duty. Allows 12 weeks unpaid leave for a "qualifying exigency" for a son, daughter, parent, or spouse on active duty.

These laws and countless others must be complied with depending on several factors. For this reason, it is important that you help your company reduce risk associated with non-compliance. A great manager has a solid understanding and overview of the various employment laws regulating employee management to mitigate risk for themselves, their employers, or their business.

CHAPTER 6

THE WARM AND FUZZY BRICK

I have always wanted to be a business owner. My desire to be a business owner started in childhood with the influence of my father. One of my fondest childhood memories was during 2nd or 3rd grade when I was about 8 or 9. My father owned a business in Brooklyn, NY, "Brown's Glass Shop" and I would come home from school and the bus let me off right in front of Dad's shop. I'll never forget the day Dad let me answer the phones, "Brown's Glass Shop, can I help you?" he'd said to answer. It was the most exciting and proud day of my life. I felt like I was a big girl... it was then that I knew I would be a business owner one day, just like Dad.

In my early 20's when I lived in the projects of Fort Greene in Brooklyn, NY, I put fliers up at the State University of NY and offered to type up resumes for $20.00 and Term Papers for $5.00 a page. I made some great side money which was so needed as a young mother of two children, the company name was "Type-Right" and I did that for about two years before I had to return to legal secretarial work. Then, in my early 30's my business dream resurfaced and I tried a few home-based businesses such as a scrapbooking company, Creative Memories (where my love of crafting flourished) and then Amway which was an amazing entrepreneurial training ground. I even used my love of crafting to go on the Holiday Craft Show circuit at local area events and made some money while enjoying my hobby.

The Amway independent business owner (IBO) model was a multi-level marketing opportunity which I enjoyed very much.

It provided a challenge for various skills sets I had yet to fully develop in my career as an employee. The Amway training model required attendance at regular conferences where IBO's were educated in sales entrepreneurship, time management, selling scripts, and so much more. I still have my arsenal of CD's. It was a training ground equivalent to the corporate structures that I had experienced up to that point in my career. The training and education in entrepreneurship were exemplary and came from great speakers like Bob Burg and Dr. Robert Rohm. But no one did sales training better than Joe Pici and his wife Dawn. Today Pici & Pici are now among the Top 10 Sales trainers in the country. During one conference, I was introduced to DISC, The Model of Human Behavior through Dr. Robert Rohm of Personality Insights, the organization from which the foundation of my DISC certification comes. I will never forget the ballroom during that conference. It was jam packed and seemed as though thousands were attendance. Dr. Rohm had come to the stage and began to present the basics of the DISC model including the key descriptors, Dominant, Inspiring, Supportive and Cautious. The descriptions and information blew me away in terms of its insights and discoveries about my family and friends but particularly about myself. His descriptions were spot on and the behaviors and communication styles and examples were incredibly accurate, I was astonished.

During one part of his presentation, he had all attendees in the ballroom stand up and as he described the natural tendencies of each style, pace, and priority, he gradually divided the attendees into each of the four behavior styles D's in one corner, I's in the other, S's and C's yet another and another. As I stood in the D section, nerves beginning to rush, I had no idea what to expect. To this point in my career, I had only attended a very few conferences where this type of active participation was required. Dr. Rohm went on with a presentation explaining more about each style and garnering laughs, chuckles, elbow pokes or pointed fingers by participants as they experienced familiarity with his explanations whether due to their own identified behaviors or that of a colleague. Next, he addressed the crown with one question and directive. "If you could be in any other quadrant or behavior style, instead of the one you are in right now, which would it be?" He then instructed the crowd to immediately point to that quadrant. Without hesitation I pointed diagonally to the S quadrant. Dr. Rohm surveyed the audience and then, to my shock, looked right at ME. I was motionless and felt my heart skip a beat, I was not much for being the center of attention as my DISC style would later confirm. He then pointed toward me and said, "you there, have we ever met before?" I felt my face flush, "No", I replied, shaking my head at the same time. He then began to describe the unique blend of DS indicating that only 17% of the population possessed it, going on to explain how the quadrants typically blend adjacent as opposed to on the diagonal. He went on to quip about when behavior styles are diagonal from each other, the individuals possessing those styles can experience internal conflict with themselves, getting chuckles from the crowd, I remember laughing at it myself. In my case, would my behavior and communication necessitate the dominant personality ready to confront due to the D behavior style or that of the Supportive, that sought peace and harmony? Can you see the dilemma? Being put on the spot, although it made me a little uncomfortable, revealed that he was spot on! At the end of his discussion, he summarized his points about the D/S blend then returned his gaze back to me and said, "you my dear are what's known as a warm and fuzzy brick". With roaring laughter, he dismissed us back to our seats. Little did I know I would embrace this label for the rest of my career, now, ever aware of the brick I would need to learn to soften.

DISC, the Model of Human Behavior changed my life in that moment. By the time Dr. Rohm had segmented the audience, everyone was disbursed throughout the ballroom in this quadrant formation.

DISC Model of Human Behavior

D DOMINANT

- Fast Paced/Outgoing
- Task Oriented
- Their Focus: Achieving Goals and Completing Tasks
- They Need: Challenges, Choices and Control.
- When Interacting: Be Direct and Get to the Point.

I INSPIRING

- Fast Paced/Outgoing
- People Oriented
- Their Focus: On People and what is Popular.
- They Need: Fun, Recognition, To be Liked.
- When Interacting: Be Excited and Interractive.

S SUPPORTIVE

- Slow Paced/Reserved
- People Oriented
- Their Focus: How to Help Others.
- They Need: Appreciation, Familiarity and Harmony
- When Interacting: Be Kind, Soft Spoken and Sincere

C CAUTIOUS

- Slow Paced/Reserved
- Task Oriented
- Their Focus: Process and Procedure
- They Need: Quality Answers, Excellence, Value
- When Interacting: Be Credible and Honest.

DISC Simple Visual - Model of Human Behavior
Image provided with permission by Dr. Robert
A. Rohm & Personality Insights, Inc.

What began twenty-four hundred years ago with scientists and philosophers, most notably Hippocrates, was the recognition of the differences in behavior that seemed to follow a pattern. Fast forward to 1928 when Dr. William Marston wrote The Emotions of Normal People after earning his doctorate from Harvard University. Marston theorized that people are motivated by four intrinsic drives that direct behavioral patterns. He then used four descriptive characteristics represented by four letters to describe a person's behavioral tendencies as Dr. Rohm did during that conference. Since then, the "DISC" concept has been used and applied in many ways. DISC profiles help you ascertain another's personality type so that you can modify your communication style to meet them at theirs which greatly improves human connection. Have you ever heard someone say, "that guy rubs me the wrong way"? That's exactly what I'm talking about in this case. Others may feel as though they do not like you, you may think you don't like others, but you must find a way to build rapport with anyone, to work or live together and find greater connection.

The model of human behavior is based on 2 foundational observations about how people normally or innately behave. PACE AND PRIORITY. We can tend to connect or completely disconnect with someone on these issues of alone. Let me explain using simple observations.

Observation #1: Some people are more fast paced, they can also be considered more outgoing, while others are slower paced, and tend to be more reserved.

Think of it as each person's "internal motor." Some people always seem ready to "go" and dive in. They engage their motor quickly. They think fast, talk fast, react fast. Others tend to engage their motor more slowly or more cautiously. They think slower and more methodically, may have slower speech patterns because they are reflecting on their thoughts and words and are slower to react. We can tend to connect or completely disconnect with someone on this issue of pace alone, which is a big mistake. The perfect example is at the mall, do the people who are taking their time irritate you? Or do the people who are zipping by you in a hurry get under your skin? That will help you identify your innate tendency for Pace.

Observation # 2: Some people are more task-oriented, while others are more people-oriented. You can think of this as each person's compass that guides them. Some people are focused on getting something done; others are more tuned-in to the people around them and their feelings.

With both observations, I want to emphasize that these behavioral tendencies are neither right nor wrong, good nor bad. They are simply different. We are simply identifying normal behavior styles. People have different styles, and that is perfectly okay. Every individual is uniquely created. In fact, everyone has a blend of all four styles at different times and in different situations. However, most people typically have 1 or 2 of these tendencies that seem to drive their everyday behavior.

When breaking down the pace and priority the DISC Model looks like this:

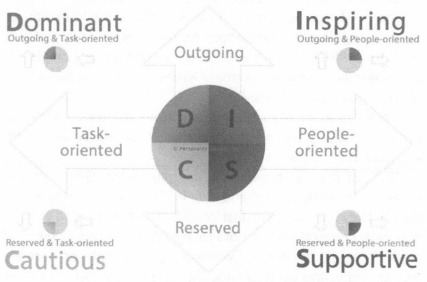

DISC Model of Human Behavior Basic Tendancies

Here are the DISC descriptors which are excerpted from Dr. Robert Rohm's DISC Basics – Your Personality Type.

D—Dominant/Direct

<u>Style</u>: They have a hard-driving, result-oriented, take-no-prisoner style. Feelings are put on the back burner—they just want the job done. Decisions are made quickly so they can move on to the next thing.

<u>How to Talk to Them:</u> The quicker, the better. Social chitchat will make their heads explode. Come prepared to your meeting, give them the details, get out of their way, and let them fly. They'll get the job done.

Here are some traits and behaviors that describe people who are comparatively high in Dominance:

- enjoy competition and challenge.
- are goal orientated and want to be recognized for their efforts.
- aim high, want authority and are generally resourceful and adaptable.
- are usually self-sufficient and individualistic.
- may lose interest in projects once the challenge has gone and they tend to be impatient and dissatisfied with minor detail.
- They are usually direct and positive with people, enjoying being the center of attraction and may take it for granted that people will think highly of them.
- They may tend to be rather critical of others. Consequently, other people may tend to see them as being rather domineering and overpowering.

Here are some traits and behaviors that describe people who are comparatively low in Dominance:

- tend to want peace and harmony.

- prefer to let others initiate action and resolve problems.
- are quiet and indirect in their approach to most situations.
- are usually cautious and calculate risks carefully before acting.
- They are generally well liked because of their mild and gentle nature. Other people will tend to see them as being patient, calm, thoughtful and a good listener.

I – Inspiring/Influencing

Style: This style of personality is a "party looking for a place to happen." They're impulsive, fun, and they love to be around people. They can be expressive, playful, and persuasive, but they can quickly lose focus.

How to Talk to Them: Diving straight into a business conversation with lots of details will bore them to death, and they'll probably stop listening. Make sure they have clear goals with deadlines, so they can keep focused. Comparatively High

Here are some traits and behaviors that describe people who are comparatively high in Influence:

- are strongly interested in meeting and being with people.
- are generally optimistic, outgoing, and socially skilled.
- are quick at establishing relationships.
- Sometimes their concern for people and people's feelings may make them reluctant to disturb a favorable situation or relationship.

Here are some traits and behaviors that describe people who are comparatively low in Influence:

- are usually socially passive.
- quite frequently have an affinity for things, machinery, and equipment.
- are generally comfortable working alone.

- frequently tend to be analytical and once they have sorted the facts out, they communicate them in a straightforward direct way.
- tend to take little at face value.
- They may well have learned and developed good social skills but they only bring these into play when logic dictates such tactics.

S - Steady/Supportive

Style: The S has never met a feeling they wanted to hurt. They are always concerned with others and avoid confrontation as if it were the Ebola virus. They are loyal, steady, and awesome team members.

How to Talk to Them: Start with friendly conversation. If you act hostile or pushy, they'll run the other way, so keep your tone even when dealing with them. When making any changes, give them time to adjust.

Here are some traits and behaviors that describe people who are comparatively high in Steadiness:

- are usually patient, calm and controlled.
- have a high willingness to help others particularly those they consider as friends.
- Generally, they can deal with the task at hand and to do routine work with patience and care.

Here are some traits and behaviors that describe people who are comparatively low in Steadiness:

- tend to enjoy change and variety in their work and non-work life.
- are expansive by nature and tend not to like routine and repetitive work/activities.
- They enjoy stretching themselves intellectually and physically.

C— Cautious/Compliant

<u>Style:</u> There is an easy way to make a C happy: Give them lots and lots of facts and details. They thrive on them. They know and follow the rules, and they're highly competent and all about business.

<u>How to Talk to Them:</u> Get right down to business with lots of facts and figures. Ask for their opinions and give them time to answer. They're great at developing procedures.

Here are some traits and behaviors that describe people who are comparatively high in Compliance/Cautious:

- are usually peaceful and adaptable.
- tend not to be aggressive.
- tend to be cautious rather than impulsive.
- avoid risk-taking.
- act in a tactful, diplomatic way and strive for a stable, ordered life.
- are comfortable following procedures in both their personal and business life.
- They prefer sticking to methods that have proved successful in the past. They have a high acceptance of rules and regulations.

Here are some traits and behaviors that describe people who are comparatively low in Compliance:

- are independent and uninhibited.
- resent rules and restrictions.
- prefer to be measured by results and are always willing to try the untried.
- Free in thought, word, and deed, they long for freedom and go to great lengths to achieve it.
- They feel that repetitive detail and routine work is best "delegated" or avoided.

We have only begun to scratch the surface of the depth and insight that the DISC Model of Human Behavior can provide. The more you learn about it and the more you interact with others with an active awareness of the innate needs of the other person, the more you will be able to connect with others in a way that is both effective and rewarding. For more information about DISC Training go to: https://thecompletemanagermakeover.com/d-i-s-c-assessments/

CHAPTER 7

BRIDGING THE GAPS IN A MULTI-GENERATIONAL WORKFORCE

I'll never forget my first visit to Miami Beach and the Fontainebleau Hotel & Resort. I took a trip with my firstborn daughter who was only about three or four years old at the time and landed in Orlando to vacation with my mother who lived there. Mom had won two free tickets on an overnight cruise boat for a day trip to Miami. We left the Port of Orlando and set sail for Miami Beach docking there overnight. It was a great day as we enjoyed the family friendly cruise offering face painting, coloring and activities for the kids and fun trivia games and opportunities for the adults to mix, mingle, laugh, and have a great time. We docked during the daytime and enjoyed overnight accommodations at the Fontainebleau. I felt like a star enjoying the large lapis pool, rock waterfall and luxurious room accommodations. I'll never forget that day. I hadn't started my hospitality career at that point, but I looked at the resort and thought how cool it would be to work in a place like this, where your office faces the beach all day long. When I finally did enter hospitality as a career it didn't take long before I remembered the Fontainebleau and set my sights on an opportunity to work there one day. I had no idea the opportunity would come within nine years of starting my hospitality career.

When that day finally arrived, driving to the hotel, I turned the corner and there it was, the "Crown Jewel" of Miami Beach, the hotel that could become the highlight of my resume. I had applied for the Director of Human Resources position and was arriving for my interview with the general manager. The regal lobby was developed with marble floors and prominent columns, photos of its history, notoriety, and prestige lined some walls of this beautifully iconic property. Members of the "rat pack" had walked these halls, Sammy Davis Jr., Frank Sinatra, Dean Martin. The hotel was visited by celebrities like Lucille Ball, Elvis Presley, Judy Garland and more. It was featured in movies like Scarface, The Bodyguard, and Goldfinger and I was here for an opportunity to work there. My dream just might come true. As I ascended the now infamous "stairway to nowhere" (which actually does go somewhere) I recalled my own Fontainebleau story when I had arrived on that small cruise boat with my mom for a trip from Orlando. Walking into the executive offices my excitement grew with both butterflies and heart palpitations but also a confidence in knowing that I was ready and wanted this opportunity. A pleasant and astute woman seated right outside the general manager's office greeted me. She reminded me of a sophisticated New York City secretary that could pleasantly greet you but keep you from seeing her boss if she wanted to. Greeting her, and introducing myself, I explained my reason for coming into her domain. She advised me to be seated and that the General Manager would be with me shortly.

Soon after, I was invited into the General Managers office. Entering the large and spacious office, I couldn't help but notice the many awards that both he and the hotel had received. The awards were reverently displayed, hanging in rows on the wall along with photos of the General Manager with familiar celebrities, presidents and sports figures peppered in for good measure. The General Manager was a mature Cuban man of distinguished presence, yet short in stature. I think this immediately connected us considering my own 4'11" frame.

As I shook his hand, he seemed surprised by its firmness and then invited me to sit across from him, his large mahogany desk between us. I selected one of the two captain's chairs and settled in for my interview. This was it, my career accomplishments now at this pinnacle. He briefly described the hotel and the position, what he was seeking and what the role required. He then sat back in his chair, cupped his hands behind his head, raised his feet upon his desk and proudly asked, "So, what makes you interested in coming to work for me?". Surprised by the question that wasn't from the HR101 playbook, I quickly took in my surroundings, assessed the situation and question, leaned in, smiled sincerely then humbly, respectfully, yet confidently replied, "well sir, with all due respect, I'm not certain that I've exactly made that decision yet". I'm not exactly certain where the reply came from, I remember simply wanting to have a mutually enjoyable conversation about my qualifications and ability to do the job. He immediately smiled at my response, maybe a bit impressed or amused by my reply. He took his hands from behind his head, lowered his feet from the desk, rolled his executive high back chair up to the desk, leaned in toward me and warmly said, "So, what would you like to know?". We proceeded to exchange information about our hospitality career experiences and he also shared a personal story about his service during the Bay of Pigs. The interview ended positively and he walked with me out of the executive office and told me they'd be in touch. The interview seemed to go very well and I left hopeful, but praying I'd be given the opportunity.

I share this story because in that defining moment, when he asked his very first interview question, there existed a generational clash between the general manager, "a Traditionalist", and me from Generation X. I didn't know it then but having now been certified as a Generational Diversity Trainer, looking back at that question and my answer, the clash was clear as day and perfectly played out. You see, Traditionalists desire that their experience and authority be respected, and the general manager had rightfully commanded and earned the respect for his numerous personal and career accomplishments. GenXers tend to politely reject authority and are confident in the knowledge, skills, and abilities they possess to get the job done or they will resourcefully figure it out.

Fortunately for me, it was a generational clash that didn't completely crash. It was an exciting moment when I received the phone call offering me the position of Director of Human Resources at the Fontainebleau Hotel and Resort. I learned many valuable lessons from that general manger and to this day continue to hold him in high esteem.

So, what is a generation and why do they clash? A generation is simply a group born during the same period who tend to share the same attributes, traits and values based on what influenced them. A generation is not necessarily defined by a person's age but rather by a generational personality that has been shaped by the events and conditions experienced during their formative years. Since each generation has its own tendencies, they each show up in the workplace with different values and views of how things should get done, there's bound to be areas where the generations will likely disagree and have conflict. The more generations in the workplace, the more conflict is likely to occur. Surveys continue to point to the fact that generation gaps make it harder to work and get things done. However, there are several factors as to why many generations are currently in the workforce. With life expectancy increasing, people are living longer and working longer, hence, prior generations remain in the workforce as new generations enter. In addition, earlier generations were expected to retire, but many people now need to remain in the workforce due to the negative economic impact of recent recessions. As a result of these things and many other factors, we have the potential of five generations in the workforce at any given time.

Generational conflict can occur at multiple junctions due to the differences between the generations. When you consider how quickly change is occurring particularly with technology, various forms of communication and the like, it's no wonder these are major areas of conflict. Let's take communication for example. Communication changed dramatically over the years. We went from having to send letters to communicate to the telegraph, the telephone quickly brought us beepers and fax machines, then there was email, mobile phones and the quickly evolving world of social media. A completely new form of communication. The same is true for information and media. We went from stagecoach, to telegraph, to newspapers, then radio, television, and now social media, which, once again, provides us with information spanning across the globe at the speed of a few keystrokes. With all this technological change in what really is a short time, it's no surprise that we are bound to have conflict regarding how information is obtained or how communication should occur in the workplace.

Let's consider the different generations, what molded and influenced them and how those influences created their generational traits. We'll also use the way each of them views institutions for comparison. Every individual within a generation is different because of the way they grew up, the influences they had at home, socioeconomic conditions, etc. This chapter isn't about putting people into a box, it's about opening that box, letting the uniqueness out and embracing what is found inside. The age bands used are those from the Pew Research Center.

The Traditionalist

Born prior to 1945, the population was about 75 million. Traditionalists spent a lot of time dealing with and experiencing many social issues. Traditionalists learned at an early age to put aside individual needs and wants and work together toward common goals. Together they won two world wars, overcame the Great Depression, built the Atomic Bomb, and sent a man to the moon. Their patriotism is beyond measure from having been raised with a "stand beside her and guide her" mentality. Traditionalists are loyal and were taught to respect authority. In the workplace, they avoid causing trouble and are good team players. They are the least likely to initiate conflict at work but also have the tendency to resist change. They value safety, security, consistency, and commitment from those around them. When you think about the formidable years experienced by this generation, keep in mind that the country lacked the social safety nets of today. There were no social security benefits, social services, or Medicare for them. Their experiences during the Great Depression created a significant "value of a dollar" mentality and the continual need to save for a rainy day. With 50%

of traditionalists being veterans and having participated in the military while winning two world wars, it is no wonder that their working style is respectful of authority. They hold steadfast to the belief that leaders lead and troops follow, which creates the "rank and file" chain of command approach to work. Traditionalists like to be recognized for their hard work and see work as a team effort. This group also tends to be technologically challenged and often struggle to learn new technology.

Traditionalists have immense faith in institutions particularly governmental institutions. During the Great Depression Franklin D. Roosevelt introduced The New Deal which put traditionalists back to work. They viewed this as their reward and recognition for their hard work during war, hence their tendency to seek the same in with workplace for career accomplishments. If you have ever enjoyed any of the beautiful US National parks like Great Smokey Mountain National Park or Mount Rushmore, or driven on roadways and traveled across bridges, then you probably have experienced the work of our traditionalist generation who built much of the infrastructure of the United States. They returned from battle to benefits such as the GI Bill so they could go to school, get an education, make a home, and start a family; and start a family they did, to the tune of 80 million children.

The Baby Boomers aka Boomers

Born between 1946 and 1964, this generation was 80 million strong in population. Boomers grew up in an era of prosperity and growth creating an extremely optimistic generation. Because of the GI bill, their traditionalist parents were able to accomplish many things during a booming post war economy that resulted in an anything is possible mentality for this generation. With an enormous increase in production of consumer goods and the promise of a good education, boomers grew up in a relatively affluent and opportunity rich world.

While graced with prosperity of the times they had to fight for much of what they wanted against the masses. In a population of 80 million, their formidable years and adulthood was wrought with competition. Boomers competed for a place in everything from a spot on a school team, a seat in their college of choice and their dream job in the workplace resulting in their incredibly competitive nature.

Career focused, competitive and with the satisfaction of achieving at work, they prefer work that makes a difference seeking to put their unique stamp on things and leave a legacy in their workplaces. They entered the workplace pushing a change in command approach and a "why do we do it this way" approach. Being competitive, they equate their worth by their status and position at work, often preferring a hierarchal work structure to establish their own place apart from the masses. Unlike their traditionalist parents, they opted for email communications over face-to-face communications, resulting in a generational clash.

Their faith in institutions was strong due to their traditionalist parents' influence so their approach to work was to work hard and stay at the same job until retirement. Having experienced the Watergate scandal, they developed a willingness to confront others, challenge the status quo and question authority, the opposite of their parents' ideals, which created clashes at home and in the workplace.

Boomers were able to have an impact in every market from the job market to the supermarket and the stock market, you name it, they had an impact. With this strength in numbers, they pushed and achieved social change in every area they could such as civil rights, women's rights', reproductive rights, and the rights of mother earth giving rise to a massive continuation in the environmental movement. Change makers they were, and that change would have definite effects on the future.

Generation X aka Gen X

Born between 1965 and 1980, this generation was significantly smaller with a population of about 46 Million. A few things occurred in the Boomer generation that impacted the size of Gen X. The women's movement attributed to this decreased population in many ways. Since women decided to reenter the workforce, they often opted to delay starting a family or not have children at all. This was made possible by the introduction of the birth control pill and passing of legislation in Roe vs. Wade.

Gen X lived during a time when the country shifted from manufacturing to servicing. With the advent of the personal computer, they grew up with technology as a normal part of their lives. Gen X experienced difficult times in their formative years and learned to live in tough times. Their childhoods were complex as they saw violence appearing on the news and close to home with AIDS, crack cocaine, missing children on milk cartons and the evolution of Mothers Against Drunk Driving. They grew up seeing every major American institution failing or called into question including the presidency (Bill Clinton/Monica Lewinsky), the military (Challenger Shuttle disaster), and organized sports (Tonya Harding/Nancy Kerrigan) resulting in a distrust of institutions and a skeptical mindset. As a result, they tend to put more faith in themselves and less faith in institutions.

They witnessed the nuclear family[10] dissolving all around them as the U.S. divorce rate tripled during their birth years, they were often raised in single-parent homes. These shifts forced Gen X to either be placed in day care or become latchkey kids[11]. As such, Gen X developed into highly individualistic and independent adults who were self-sufficient and flexible. They began the shift in balancing work and home life because they saw the institutions that their parents worked so hard for crumble and along with them the financial security they once expected. In the workplace, they worked hard to carve out their own identity from larger Boomer generation. They crave responsibility and politely reject authority and fixed work schedules. They were the first to take advantage of technology and incorporate it into their work. Because of the economic boom of the 90's and their smaller

---

[10] a family group consisting of a man, a woman, and their children.

[11] a child who was at home without adult supervision during some part of the day, typically after school until a parent returned from work.

workforce population, they could say "show me the money" in the workplace.

The skeptical independent GenXers are now thrown into the mix with loyal Traditionalists and optimistic Boomers. In addition, consider the Traditionalist "chain of command" mentality confronted by the Boomers "change of command" mindset, and layer in Gen X with their independent "self-command" approach, you are bound to have some clashes. Now enter...

Generation Y aka Millennials

Born between 1981 and 1996 this population was almost as large as the Boomers with 76 million.

Millennials have a mix of the Traditionalist loyalty, Boomers' optimism and just enough of the Gen X skepticism to be cautious.

Achievement-oriented and confident, they are a realistic generation of problem solvers and social supporters.

They don't know what it is to be without a computer, cell phone or any other electronic devices.

Millennials are realistic about challenges of modern life for a modern kid. Forget the kid missing on the milk carton, they are worried about the missing classmate from the desk next to theirs because of gunshots and terror at home as they witnessed events like Columbine, Virginia Tech; and Sandy Hook Elementary School. They are directly affected by these violent outbreaks, the readily available illegal drugs in their communities and the proliferation of gangs. Millennials site "personal safety" as their number one workplace issue.

The optimistic Boomers have a stronger resemblance to their parents which results in their feeling of empowerment to take positive action when things go wrong. These same parents wanted to ensure that their millennial children didn't have the same challenges they did growing up, having to compete for the spot in school, the spot on the playground, the spot at work so we began to see the "everyone gets a participation trophy" philosophy. Their parents were also highly communicative, participation-oriented parents, so Millennials are often included in major family decisions since they are old enough to point. From deciding where to go on family vacations to what personal computer to purchase in their home, Millennials have always been part of the day-to day negotiation of their home lives. It's no wonder they have similar expectations in the workplace, expecting they'll be able to contribute and collaborate right from the start. They value family over work, are not happy with working long hours, and look for flexible schedules to achieve real work life balance.

Millennials are prone to communicating electronically and rely on technology to do their jobs. They prefer using the internet as a means of learning and making purchases and have been inundated with information, music, and media on a minute-by-minute basis. They had access to this technology as a normal part of life at an early age. They saw the expansion of media and the internet that broke down walls physically when the Berlin Wall fell, and figuratively because now they could see or hear what was happening globally in the worldwide web. With this access to answers and information a few keystrokes away, gone were the days of visiting the local library or grabbing an encyclopedia to learn new things.

So, the Traditionalist came of age in the workforce in a "chain of command" environment and the Boomers were focused on "change of command" the Gen X fought for "self-command", so what do you think about the Millennials? Well, they entered the workforce and said, "don't command – collaborate!" But now, here comes...

Generation Z aka Gen Z

Born after 1996, the population is estimated at 57 million members according to the U.S. Department of Education. While the majority of Gen Z are the children of Generation X, they are the first generation birthed by the three generations that came before them resulting in a far more diverse generation on multiple levels. With access to mobile technology since they were crawling, Gen Z is known for being tech savvy, but more than technology, this generation is also shaped by continuing crises such as: the rise of school shootings, climate change, terrorism, and the Great Recession. These events make Gen Z more cautious and pragmatic, but they have also inspired this generation to be world changers. Their concept of family is more diverse with the nuclear family representing only about 46% of American households. More often gender roles overlap as their generation has experienced more stay-at-home fathers than ever before.

Gen Z is more socially aware, feel responsible for creating change in the world and are more socially concerned than any other previous generation. They often seek organizations whose missions include an opportunity for them to contribute to a local or global community. Raised to be competitive during the most disruptive era, they like the idea of being in control of their own destinies. They are extremely politically savvy and know that anything is possible in the Presidency. There is a lot more interest in understanding the political landscape and they saw huge regulatory shifts in healthcare, the legalization of gay marriage and medical marijuana. With 20 something billionaire entrepreneurs and watching people make a living creating YouTube videos, it's not surprising this generation exhibits a lot of entrepreneurial tendencies.

Only time will tell how this generation will be viewed historically but their influence may very well be unlike any other.

A few words about Cuspers

Cuspers are an important group as they can identify with more than one generation for various reasons. That's my case, I am a Cusper. I tend to place myself right between Gen X and the Boomer Generation because I entered the workforce at 16 years old and stayed there. I was very much aware of the world of work, the social norms and watched but also participated in the competitiveness of the boomer generation. I find myself right in that middle as I had that early entry into the workforce but in my earlier teens and formidable years, I was totally a latchkey kid. Cuspers can play an important role in the workplace, they are great at mediating, explaining, and resolving conflicts because they can relate to both generations that may be clashing.

No matter what generation you are from, one is not better or worse than another, they are simply different. What will you do with this new insight and information? You are a bit more aware of some of the clash points but also you understand the reason behind them to help you navigate them better, not just avoid them, but to reduce them. Maybe you've already had some exposure to this conversation, maybe not. Hopefully, this will allow you to be more open-minded when dealing with other generations as you know have a bit more information about their different perspective.

Generations in the Workplace

**Gen-Z
Gen Edge**

- **Population:** approx. 65 Million
- **Birth Years:** approx 1996-2010
- **Defining Moments:** Great Recession, "Obama-Care", Gay Marriage, Medical Marijuana and Still Happening
- **Positive Attributes:** Open Minded, Creative, Entrepreneurial
- **Traits:** Inquisitive, Industrious, hesitant to take risks with stockmarket, fiscally conscious,

**Gen-Y
Millenials**

- **Population:** 80 Million
- **Birth Years:** 1982-1993
- **Defining Moments:** Challenger Disaster, 9/11, Oklahoma City Bombing, School Violence, Clinton/Lewinsky, Multicultural, TV talk shows
- **Positive Attributes:** Multi-taskers, Fearless, Worldly, Desire to make a difference.
- **Traits:** Tolerant, self-sufficient, socially/politically conscious; Globally concerned, Cyber/Tech literate Realistic, Environmentally conscious

Gen-X

- **Population:** 58.5 Million
- **Birth Years:** 1965-1981
- **Defining Moments:** Nixon Resigns, Energy Crisis, High Divorce Rate, Cold War, Technology Revolution, Stock Market Crash, Corp. Downsizing, Fall of Berlin Wall, Desert Storm, Rodney King and L.A riots.
- **Positive Attributes:** Critical thinkers, Multi-taskers, Question the Status Quo
- **Traits:** Pragmatic, self-sufficient, Skeptical especially of institutions, Entrepreneurial, Resourceful, self-reliant, adaptive, independent

**Baby
Boomers**

- **Population:** 79.9 Million
- **Birth Years:** 1946-1964
- **Defining Moments:** TV, Civil Rights Movement, Prosperity, Family planning, JFK, MLK and RFK assassinated, Woodstock, Vietnam, Rock and roll.
- **Positive Attributes:** Social change
- **Traits:** Idealistic, breaks the rules, time stressed, politically correct; Competitive, questioners of authority, desiring to put their own stamp on institutions, the sandwiched generation, optimistic.

**Traditionalists
Silent
Generation**

- **Population:** 46.5 Million
- **Birth Years:** Prior to 1946
- **Defining Moments:** Stock market crash, Great Depression, FDR and the New Deal, Pearl Harbor
- **Positive Attributes:** Calm, historians
- **Traits:** Conservative, disciplinarians, respect for authority, loyal, patriotic; desire to leave a legacy; Fiscally Conservative; faith in institutions.

Generations in the Workplace

CHAPTER 8

LOW COST/NO COST ENGAGEMENT, RECOGNITION AND REWARDS

The engagement ideas shared here aren't rocket science, they are shared with the expectation that at a minimum your organization offers locally competitive wages, minimal health benefit and provides a comfortable, pleasant work environment. If your employees are melting because your AC hasn't worked for 5 years, don't worry about these ideas, spend the time, save these pennies, and call an HVAC technician. Notwithstanding those things, you certainly can look at ways to create an engaging workplace and there is a plethora of things that can be done. Hopefully, these ideas will get you to think or re-think how you engage, incentivize, and reward your employees.

Let's first define engagement. We've heard this buzz phrase "employee engagement" for decades. It means to hold the attention of, or to induce to participate. Quantum Workplace defines employee engagement as "the strength of the mental and emotional connection employees feel toward their places of work", Gallup says, engaged employees are "those who are involved in, enthusiastic about, and committed to their work and workplace" and according to Willis Towers Watson, employee engagement is "employees' willingness and ability to contribute to company success". Engagement seeks a mutually beneficial, two-way collaborative environment.

For several years organizations such as Gallup and others have written dozens of articles with sobering headlines such as, "Majority of American Workers Not Engaged in Their Jobs." As business owners, employers, and managers, we should find that very disturbing. In a particular survey, Gallup found that 70% of a team's engagement is influenced by managers and yet another article, supported by yet another survey found that only 1/3 of workers are enthusiastic about the work they do and feel they are contributing to their organizations in positive way. If you are reading this book next to or near two other people, one of you is not enthusiastic about the work you do. Now you may think that it's money on workers' minds, and that is partially true but it's not the only reason the American workforce is disengaged. This disengagement issue spans decades, in that, a survey conducted by The American Psychological Association (APA) dated March 8, 2011 provides these insights:

This survey found workers reported discontentment because of:

- limited opportunities for growth or advancement (43%),
- heavy workload (43%),
- unrealistic expectations (40%),
- and long hours (39%).

Additionally,

- less than half of employees (43 percent) said they receive adequate non-monetary rewards and recognition for their contributions at work.
- only 57 percent reported being satisfied with their employer's work-life practices and
- according to Time Magazine almost 80% of employees believe they get no respect at work.

Fast forward a decade plus and we still have Gallup's State of the Global Workplace indicate that 85% of Employees Are Not Engaged in the Workplace which in turn means only 15 percent of employees are engaged.

Ok so we have some facts but, why engage? The work seems to be getting done, right? According to Fortune Magazine, companies listed on the *100 Best Places to Work* list, (over a 10-year period) showed 30-40% more profitability than the companies listed on the S&P 500 (which is the market index of the top 500 publicly traded American companies). Of the 100 Best Places to Work employee recognition and engagement practices were a critical component of these companies business philosophies and cultures. To top that, Gallup estimated that worker disengagement accounts for more than $300 billion annually in lost productivity in the U.S. alone. If these aren't reasons to engage your workforce then what is? So, how do we engage?

The good news is that most workers don't need a high-priced award to feel appreciated. Even if you don't have a lot of money in the budget, there are still ways to treat your employees right and show appreciation for the extra effort. In a major long-term study, published in *Corporate Culture and Performance*[12] companies that had the best corporate cultures, that encouraged all-around leadership initiatives and that highly appreciated their employees, customers, and owners, grew 682 percent in revenue while those without performance enhancing cultures showed a revenue growth of only 166%. While these statistics are remarkable, I think it is more important to create cultures that treat humans in humane ways, and value kindness, empathy, respect, compassion, patience, self-discipline, humor, and gentleness. When we begin to exude those virtues more in the workplace therein lies a culture of humanness and engagement. Here are some great ways to engage for No or Low Costs.

No Cost Engagement is free yet PRICELESS.

- Smile. Mother Teresa says that it is a beautiful thing when we smile at sometime, it is actually an act of love that we express to that person.

---

[12] Kotter, J. P. (2008). Corporate Culture and Performance. United Kingdom: Free Press.

- Employees have names. Use them. Make it a point to know all the names in your department and business or sneak a nametag peek if you have too. We've heard from Dale Carnegie that that the most important sound and the sweetest thing we can hear is the sound of our own name.
- Hold regular Rap/Communication or Listen In Sessions (take an employee for coffee, a walk or just to the water cooler. Learn about them through asking questions about their career goals, dreams, family, their suggestions for improvement or if they have what they need to do the job. Take notes about what they said and then see how you might implement change because of their suggestions. Just listen to them, learn about them, engage with them.
- Collect information about them so you know more about their likes. I used what I call an "Engage Me!" form. I added it to new hire paperwork or rolled it out as a new initiative where I would have all employees list their favorite things– color – sports team, hobbies, holiday, flavor (sour, sweet, chocolate), books/author, favorite foods, or thing to do outside work, etc. When it came time to reward or recognize them in some way, I knew what their specific interests were and could tailor the recognition accordingly because nothing is worse than presenting a box of chocolate only to find out that the employee is allergic.
- Institute a way for employees to recognize each other. Ask coworkers to write something they admire about an employee on a heart shaped piece of paper, tell them it's Valentine's day every day and send some coworker admiration. Frame their message along with a photo of the employee and hang them along the hallways for all to see. I once used simple Lifesavers® candy rolls in a recognition program to tell someone how much of a Lifesaver they were for staying late, picking up a shift or working a double. It was a simple program but one that made a major impact in our employee relations culture and morale.

- Embark on a partnership with a company called Tickets at Work. With FREE online access for your company, they offer your employees Exclusive Discounts, Special Offers, Access to Preferred Seating & many other special perks for thousands of offerings including theme parks, shows, restaurants, sporting events, concerts, movie tickets and much more.

- Send E-cards which are fun and easy to send with many of the large card companies, but remember, nothing can ever replace a thoughtful handwritten sentiment and thank you. I used to use a handwritten note stamped with my favorite Marvin the Martian Stamp as my signature. It didn't take long for the buzz to begin about where that little stamped card or note came from. Surprise, from HR! Eventually, they knew it came from me when they see Marvin. There are two small words that can deliver the highest ROI when it comes to employee incentives and they're "THANK YOU".

- Create a VIP parking spot. Reserve one of the best spots in the parking lot for employees who have done something outstanding. Rotate VIP parking privileges each month.

- Host a State of the Company address to let your workforce know a lot more than is often shared such as goals, strategies, highs, lows, customer feedback. This helps them truly feel a connection to your organization and part of the team rather than a worker bee.

- Launch a voluntary Health/Wellness campaign to boost camaraderie such as an American Cancer Society Great American Smoke-out campaign, typically held in November. The society has all the necessary materials to launch a company-wide initiative for free. Not only will it boost morale and foster a sense of competition but it may also save lives. I quit smoking in 2009 because of a Great American Smoke-out Campaign. You can rally around any cause or rotate them quarterly. Solicit feedback on local or national organizations that your workforce may want to support, list them all and have employees vote on the charity to support that quarter.

- Get the team together for social and community projects to build morale, promote a sense of inclusion and focus on corporate responsibility. There was no time more rewarding than to gather employees for a Relay for Life or a Habitat for Humanity Project. Volunteermatch.org is a great place to start or simply search for non-profits in your area and find out how you can support them specifically with the gift of time.
- You can also give employees time on the job to take part in free webinars offered in their specialty through your local chamber or give them upskill time using the FREE Microsoft Office Suite tutorials that can be found at http://office.microsoft.com/en-us/training/FX100565001033.aspx

Low-Cost Engagement

- Your local chamber or offices of small and economic business development may offer Education and Training valuable to your employees. Why not consider giving select employees their choice of one session per quarter to attend for their continuing development. You can also choose to host the business or personal development workshops that give employees knowledge, skills, and abilities relevant to their personal or professional life.
- Offer an extra day or half day off with pay for a job well done.
- Cater in a lunch or order in Pizza for the team as a surprise during any day of the week.
- Visit your local bagel shop one morning and bring in breakfast. It's a small and simple gesture that everyone will enjoy and a low-cost way to show your appreciation.
- If you have a break room, no matter how small, get employees involved to create an official name for your Cafeteria, give it a facelift with $100.00 worth of paint and some affordable artwork, or better yet have your employees make the artwork, you just provide some canvas and paint. Have an official grand opening celebration to show off their work and the new space.

- Allow employees to take family or affinity days. For those days when kids may be off school or have early release, allow employees to work from home if that is an option. Whether it's a school half day or snow day, let employees skip the commute and spend more time with their kids, while getting work done, we've certainly seen in these last few years that remote work is here to stay.

- Celebrate Holidays in your cafeteria or break room and have inexpensive decorations and distribute Holiday Facts and information on the history of the day. I use the National Day Calendar to find fun things to celebrate every day! Since we have founded National Management Training week, you can purchase your own calendar at https://www.idevaffiliate.com/33275/135.html

- Turn the break room into a game room. You may not beat GOOGLE but stock the break room with some classic and quick games like Connect 4, playing cards, Boggle and Scrabble which can be left out for others to continue the game. Checkers can be played relatively quickly and trivial pursuit game cards can be left out for some lunchtime interaction and trivia.

- Give a Discount on the products or services you sell. Encourage employees to pass the offer along to friends and family. It's a partnership that benefits everyone.

- Purchase scented candles and add a notecard that says, "You Brighten Our Day!"

- Buy Payday Candy bars and give them out during your next payday.

- Give out M&M Candy packets with a note that says, "Thanks for being so Motivated & Marvelous", or come up with your own M words.

- Bring in some wrapped cinnamon buns to say, "Thank you for Working your buns off" and if that's too risqué just pick up some cupcakes and tell your employees "You take the cake!"

Recognition doesn't have to be expensive or elaborate, employees at all levels of the organization want and need to make a human connection, to know they are appreciated. To assess your engagement processes, conduct annual engagement surveys, identify your engagement processes if you have them and see what your employees think about those processes, then set a course of action for improvement. I hope these Low Cost and No Cost ideas provide a great start.

AFTERWORD

The Complete Manager Makeover has taken a full circle approach to your role in human resources and people management. From the Fundamental Philosophies that are some of my own foundational principles of leadership and management to the basics of human resources compliance, we certainly have covered a lot. The P.R.I.D.E.S. Model of Interviewing provides a solid framework to help you engage your prospective employees more efficiently, with the intent of not only improving the quality of hire, but also ensuring there is a mutual fit. We've discussed the importance of training adult learners with an effective Know, Show, Do Review process, but also explained how differently people learn and the need to value the knowledge, ideas, and experiences that our trainees bring to the table. We've covered the performance review process, it's pitfalls and best practices along with ways to succeed at correcting behavior and providing feedback and ensuring that we do so at regular intervals, to improve the chances of employee success, and your success as a manager. Hopefully, this book has also begun to equip you to conduct the various conversations you may face and give you answers for the "what do I say" problem. We've touched on the legalities and shared some information about the various federal laws with which you must comply to equip you to know when help might be needed.

Most importantly, we talked about the D.I.S.C. Model of Human Behavior, the human intrinsic drives that can improve your ability to connect with others whether at home or at work. We also focused on understanding the various generations and the experiences that shaped their world views which sought to provide a new perspective of those around you, no matter what their age.

No one of these chapters should be implemented without the other, the employee life cycle is a complete process, a circle that has a beginning and an end. To remove any one part would not offer a complete approach to manage employees efficiently, effectively, and humanly. I hope the checklists, guides and toolkit have been helpful, providing practical tools and skills for you to manage employees in your day-to-day responsibilities. The way you communicate with employees helps to increase engagement and retention and improve your overall performance as a leader in your organization. Yet, it will be up to you to implement the new skills, suggestions, and strategies, to improve the human connection, hire, train, develop and motivate employees, while also reducing risk for yourself and your organizations.

After new knowledge is obtained you have a choice to make. You can choose to do nothing with the knowledge and in so doing, you've just wasted your time, or you can put the knowledge into practice on a regular basis. That is when you accomplish change and true transformation. I've heard it said that "knowledge is power", but I prefer the "Knowledge in ACTION is Power" mindset. So, now you have the knowledge, but only the actions you take will give you the Power to become a great manager.

I encourage you to visit thecompletemanagermakeover.com for more resources, E-Books, or ongoing training support so that together we can continue Transforming the Human in Human Resources®.

APPENDIX

Sample Rap Session Form

Employee Name: _____ Date _____
Manager Name: _____Next Meeting _____

This documentation should be used as a tool for obtaining employee feedback, coaching, counseling, continuous improvement, and recognition.

Suggested items for discussion:

1. Employee Satisfaction
2. Does employee have sincere, specific appreciation or recognition for another individual or group.
3. Provide sincere, specific appreciation or recognition to employee.
4. Guest/Customer Satisfaction (Are Guest Service Standards Being Practiced? (list those standards here)
5. Career Progression/Personal Interests/Development (Goals, Training Opportunities, Internal Interests):
6. Performance Feedback (Is Feedback Regular enough, are there additional training needs, does employee have suggestions for coworkers or management.
7. Suggestions for process improvement in any area.
8. New Ideas
9. Understanding. Asking questions like "Why do we...?" or "Why don't we...?" creates opportunities to discover areas for Improvement or better understanding of processes.
10. Core Company Culture Discussion/Reinforcement
11. Wish List – Surfacing future desires within the operation or aspirations for the future.

Sample Behavior Based Interview Questions and More

The following questions will help you determine if the candidate:

- Can understand multiple questions.
- Can ask for clarification if needed.
- Can explain bridges between jobs.
- Logically moved from one job to the next.
- Can describe his or her understanding of an accomplishment.

Questions:

- What are the strongest skills you feel you would bring to this position (based on past work and other roles)?
- What have you liked least about past positions?
- What have you liked most about past positions?
- Do you have special training you feel would set you apart from other candidates?
- If you had to rank your computer literacy (e- mail, word processing, windows, etc.) on a scale of 1-5, what would it be? Where are your strengths in this area?
- Tell me about a time you had a problem to solve. What was the nature of the problem, what was your approach to solving the problem?
- Have you worked in a team environment before?
- Have you managed employees, been a team leader or project leader in past positions? Tell me about how you managed the team?
- Tell me about a time you were under extreme pressure, what was the situation and how did you manage the pressure?
- What are your career plans over the next two years?
- What about this position is of interest to you?
- Why are you interested in a job/career change at this time?
- What salary range are you looking for/expecting? Work Schedule?

Customer Service

- What are the steps involved in successfully handling an irate customer?
- Tell me about how you have handled a dissatisfied client/customer in the past, what was the nature of their dissatisfaction, how did it get resolved? Were they satisfied with the result? How do you know?
- Tell me about your experience in dealing with the public.
- Has a salesperson ever come in or called to talk to your boss without an appointment, how did you handle the salesperson?
- Give us an example of a situation you handled exemplifying superior customer service?
- Have you ever had to deal with a client/customer who used abusive language? What did you do?
- Tell me about the most you've ever done to obtain information to better understand an internal/external customer. What did you do? How did the information improve your service?
- What have you done to educate customers about your company/product/service capabilities?
- To satisfy internal/external customers, we sometimes promise more than we can deliver. Tell me about a time when you over committed yourself or your company. What happened? What would you do differently?
- How have you known if your internal/external customers were satisfied? Give me an example of a customer you know was satisfied because of your efforts.
- Tell me about your most difficult customer. Describe a specific interaction you had with this customer.
- Sooner or later, we all must deal with an internal/external customer who makes unreasonable demands. Think of a time when you had to handle an unreasonable request. What did you do?

- Describe a time when you effectively handled an internal/external complaint.
- Can you describe a time when you didn't handle an internal/external customer complaint well? What did you do? What happened?
- Occasionally we wish we could change how we interacted with an internal/external customer. Tell me about a recent interaction that you wish you had handled differently.

Decision Making

- What type of decisions do you make in your current position?
- What decisions are easiest for you to make and which ones are the most difficult? Why?
- What steps are involved in your decision-making process? Give me an example.
- What items of information do you typically need before you make a decision?
- Think about an occasion when you needed to choose between two or three seemingly equally viable paths to accomplish a goal. How did you make your decision about the path to follow?
- Describe the process you followed to pick the college you attended.
- When you are working with a coworker or reporting staff member, how do you decide upon and communicate the points at which you need feedback and progress reports?

Effective Communications

- What is your method to ensure you effectively communicate with others?
- What are some rules to follow to insure effective communications with your co-workers?
- What means of communication may be used to effectively establish a new policy?

- Communicating with your supervisor is an important aspect of all our jobs. In addition to being brief, what guidelines do you follow to communicate effectively with your supervisor?

Experience and Education

- How does your experience and education qualify you for this job?
- What aspect of your education applies to this position?
- What training have you received that qualifies you for this job?
- What have you done outside of formal education to develop yourself?
- How do you stay current on new trends, updates, and information in your field/industry?
- What training opportunities have you taken advantage of and why?
- Tell us about yourself and focus on aspects of your experience that apply specifically to the position that you're applying for.
- How does your current job qualify you for this position?
- How does your experience qualify you for this job?
- Describe a typical day at your present position.
- What were your three greatest accomplishments on your last job? What do you think were the critical factors that helped you achieve them?
- What are some of the things on your current job you have done well?
- What is the most difficult assignment you have had?
- What accomplishment on the job are you the proudest of? Why?
- Tell me about a time you made significant contributions to the operation of your work group or company? What were the contributions and why were they the focus?
- What makes you more qualified than other candidates?

- Why do you want to leave your current job?
- What actions have you taken in the past 5 years to prepare you for this position?
- What steps have you taken in the past two years to improve your qualifications?
- In areas where you fell short on qualifications for previous positions, what steps did you take to make up for the shortfall?
- Recall an incident where you made a major mistake. What was the mistake and what did you do after the mistake was made? What did you learn from this mistake?
- What is the greatest failure you've had? What would you have done differently?
- Tell us about a difficult situation that you encountered and how you resolved it.

First Job

- How has your education prepared you for this position?
- Which courses will contribute the most to your effective performance in this job?
- What was the single most important lesson that you have learned in school?
- What do you like the most about the career you are seeking?
- What do you like least about the career you are seeking?
- Why did you choose the college that you attended?
- Why did you select the major that you selected?

Judgment

- Tell me about a time when you displayed integrity. What was the situation?
- Tell us about a situation where you made a mistake. How did you handle the mistake and what was the resolution?
- Give me a situation that illustrates your ability to exercise good judgment.

Learning

- In any new job there are some things we pick up quickly and other things that take more time to learn. In your last job, tell me about something you learned quickly and something that took more time. What could you have done differently to expedite learning?
- What tricks or techniques have you learned to make your job easier or yourself more effective? Give me an example of a few techniques.
- It's never easy to fully understand everything about a new product, service, or procedure, even after attending a training session. Can you give me an example of when this happened to you? What did you do to ensure you learned the new process?
- Tell me about your greatest learning challenge a time when you had to learn a great deal in a short amount of time. How did you ensure learning occurred?

Motivation

- Name some of the ways that a supervisor can motivate staff.
- What motivates you?
- Tell us about a situation where you motivated your staff or co-workers to extraordinary accomplishments.

New Job

- What is the most/least attractive aspect of the job you are interviewing for?
- To successfully meet the responsibilities of this position, which of your personal qualities will be of the greatest benefit?
- What aspect of our organization has the greatest appeal for you?
- Knowing our organization and the position you are interviewing for, where do you think can you make the greatest contribution?

- How will the job you are interviewing for fit into your career plans?
- Why are you interested in the position?
- What are you seeking from this job/career?
- What challenges do you think that you will face in moving from your current position to this position?
- In comparison to your current position, what do you think will be different in your new position?

Personal Qualities

- Give me an example of your analytical abilities.
- Tell me about a particularly difficult problem that you analyzed and what was your recommendation?
- How confident are you that you can successfully perform the duties of this position and why?
- Tell me about a situation that would demonstrate the level of confidence that you have in yourself.
- Tell me about a situation that would demonstrate the level of confidence a previous manager had in you.
- Tell me about a situation that would show the confidence your coworkers have in you.
- Describe a past situation where you came up with a creative solution to a problem.
- Provide me with an example of your ability to work independently.
- What experience have you had in pressure situations?
- Tell me about your most stressful day. What made it stressful? How did the day end?
- Provide me with an example of how you've asserted yourself in an emergency or high-pressure situation.
- Briefly describe the most significant responsibility you have had in your career and what it taught you?
- Name the greatest risk you have taken which resulted in failure.

Planning and Organizing

- How have you avoided scheduling conflicts when working on a project with several other people?
- What types of scheduling have you done on your job? Give me an example of something you've recently had to schedule.
- Prioritizing projects/activities/responsibilities can be challenging. Tell me about the last time you could've done a better job of prioritizing a project/activity/responsibility. What happened?
- What have you done to make your department/group/team more efficient or organized? Give me an example.
- Deadlines can't always be met. Tell me about a time when you missed a deadline on a project. What were the causes?
- Have you planned any conferences, workshops, or retreats? Describe the steps involved in planning one of these.
- Prioritizing sales calls and activities can be challenging. Tell me about the last time you could have done a better job of prioritizing. What happened?
- Describe how you have organized materials (files, records, or other information) so that you could find them easily.
- Describe how you plan your daily or weekly activities. Walk me through the process you used for planning yesterday or last week.
- Do you have a particular system for organizing your work area? Tell me about a time when that system helped you in your job and a time when it didn't.
- Describe a situation in which someone needed files or records from you. How were your materials organized so that you could retrieve them?

Problem Solving

- Provide me with an example of your problem-solving ability.
- What are the essential elements of effective problem solving?

- Tell me about a situation in which you were required to analyze and solve a complex problem. What was the result?

Strengths and Opportunities

- Why should we hire you?
- What can you contribute to our organization?
- We have interviewed several highly qualified applicants for this position. What sets you apart from the others?
- What are your greatest strengths and how have they helped you to succeed?
- What have you done to focus on your own personal and professional development?

Teamwork

- Tell me about an unsuccessful team of which you were a member. What, if anything, could you have done differently?
- Tell me about a successful team of which you were a member. What was the most outstanding characteristic of that team? What did you contribute?
- What are the important qualities a person should have to become an effective employee?
- What qualities do you have that make you an effective team player?
- Do you work better by yourself or as part of a team?
- What can you contribute to establish a positive working environment for our team?
- What type of people do you work best with?
- Name some of the pitfalls to be avoided in building an effective team.
- Tell me about a time when you had to assemble a project team. What factors did you taken into consideration when assembling that team?
- What actions have you taken in the past as a supervisor to establish teamwork in the department/organization?

- To accomplish goals, a team often must obtain resources from other areas. Tell me about a time when you had to do this. What did you do? How did you know your actions benefited the team?
- Tell me about two different teams in which you have been involved and describe the different roles you performed on each.
- For a team to function effectively, every member must be committed to the team and its goals. Tell me about a time you demonstrated your commitment to a team. What were the results?
- Sharing information is critical to organizational success. Can you think of a time when important information wasn't shared? What happened? What have you done to ensure it doesn't happen again?

Working Effectively With Others

- Tell me about a time you had to deal with conflict? How did you go about finding resolution?
- Recall a time you had a conflict with a supervisor. What was the nature of the conflict, how did you go about resolving it? Who was wrong and why?
- In what kinds of situations do you find it most difficult to deal with people?
- Describe to me the extent to which you have worked with executives or top management.
- Tell me about your experience in dealing with a variety of different people.
- Working with people can be a real challenge sometimes. Can you tell me about a time when you had problems working with someone? What did you do? What happened?
- Give me an example of a person with whom you find it difficult to get along. Why?

Corrective Action Checklist

Before Documenting

☐ Is there support for the action through witnesses?

☐ Meet with witnesses before taking corrective action.

☐ Obtain the actual physical evidence and information essential to the Company's case before taking corrective action; e.g., copies of timecards/records documents.

☐ Review any information you already have regarding the employee.

☐ Has the employee received notice (should prior feedback be given) – Am I sure the employee understood this notice?

☐ If prior documentation given, has the employee had sufficient time to correct the problem?

☐ Have I taken all-possible action steps to attempt to salvage the employee - (training, transfer, leave of absence, part-time)?

☐ Is corrective action consistent with the past practice?

☐ Did I consider employee's point of view, personal difficulties, or mitigating circumstances?

☐ Corrective action should not be a surprise.

☐ Have I reviewed my actions with my supervisors, HR, or ownership?

Before the Meeting

☐ Properly complete the documentation, ensure necessary backup is included.

☐ Ensure HR or another senior executive reviews the document whenever possible to ensure:
  • Consistency of application
  • Appropriate verbiage

☐ Arrange to meet with the employee privately. Do not reprimand an employee in public or in front of others. Ensure uninterrupted time.

☐ Prepare for the meeting by reviewing your notes and files about both the specific incident or problem in question and any past corrective action taken, either verbal or written.

☐ Anticipate any questions the employee might have.

During the Meeting

☐ Explain to the employee why you have called the meeting if the employee is unaware.

☐ State the specific problem in terms of actual performance and desired performance.

☐ Explain what steps have been taken already and what the next step may be in future.

☐ Give the employee a chance to respond, explain, and defend his or her actions. Let them talk but keep them on the subject at hand.

☐ Acknowledge the employee's statements.

☐ Tell the employee that you expect his or her behavior to improve. Give specific examples and suggestions.

☐ Indicate your confidence in the employee's ability and willingness to improve.

☐ Have the employee confirm that he or she understands the problem and is clear on expectations.

☐ Reassure the employee that you value his/her work and are committed to their improvement.

After the Meeting

☐ If written documentation has been issued, be sure to give the employee the opportunity to sign any documentation for the file and provide comments or ask questions.

☐ Give the employee a copy of the document, after they or a witness has signed.

☐ Monitor the employee's behavior and performance to make sure that the problem has been corrected.

☐ Original is placed in the employee's employment file.

☐ There should be no disciplinary documentation in an employee's file of which the employee is unaware.

Finally, ensure you have checked the employee's file for previous infractions that should be included in this documentation. Be sure the notice clearly outlines the future expectations regarding behavior/performance? Determine if the disciplinary measure will potentially limit a recurrence?

When your documentation is prepared you can begin the corrective action conversation. The corrective action conversation consists of outlining the nature of the unacceptable performance, getting the buy in from the employee that the behavior is a problem, discussing the consequences as well as solutions.

Disciplinary Process Checklist

1. Is the problem serious enough to implement the disciplinary process?
2. Is this an objective, fact-based action rather than subjective, emotion-based action?
3. Have you investigated all unusual or mitigating circumstances?
4. Does your documentation clearly support your perception of poor performance or disruptive behaviors?
5. Does your documentation establish a legally defensible position?
6. Have you properly addressed the removal of barriers or the allocation of resources affecting this employee's performance?
7. Are you treating this employee as consistently as others in the company's present or past employment?
8. Have you investigated if this employee has any right to claims of unfair treatment or circumstance?
9. Have all proper procedures and guidelines been followed as established by the human resources department?
10. Have you addressed all reasonable options for helping the employee improve his/her performance behavior problems?
11. Have all influential parties been consulted and their support obtained prior to beginning the disciplinary process (your manager, human resources department, legal counsel, others)?

12. Have all employment and collective bargaining agreements, as well as any contractual procedures, been carefully reviewed and considered prior to beginning the disciplinary process?
13. Does the employee understand the job requirements? Does the employee know where s/he has fallen short?
14. Have you determined whether the organization has support for the action through witnesses?
15. If so, have you met with those witnesses before taking corrective action?
16. Have you obtained the actual physical evidence and information essential to the company's case before taking corrective action; e.g., copies of sick leave record?
17. If the employee has received prior notice – are you sure the employee understood that notice?
18. Has the employee had sufficient time to correct the problem?

The Effective Termination Process

When an employee leaves the organization because of the disciplinary process, due to resignation or termination, the following guidelines should be followed:

- A witness is highly suggested during all potential separation events.
- Preserve the employee's dignity. (No matter how disrespectful or abusive the employee is, always remain professional.)
- Maintain confidentiality forever. (Just because the employee is gone does not absolve you of your responsibility.)
- Do not permit the employee to return to the facility. (There are significant security considerations for you, your co-workers and other management personnel.)
- Express your regret over the outcome. Do not apologize.

When the employee is terminated, you may want to consider offering outplacement assistance in seeking a new job. Training and assistance with interviewing, networking or resume writing may be extremely helpful and seen by others as a humane gesture by the organization. It is in your best interest to help the dismissed employee find employment.

All requests for employment references from potential future employers for your separated problem employees should be referred to the Human Resources department or upper management. You could be considered legally liable for any detrimental statements.

Preparing For The Termination Discussion

1. **Review the reasons for the termination.**
   Make certain that:

   - All incidents of below-standard performance have been noted in specific and measurable terms and that it's clear that performance standards have not been met on several occasions.
   - There is verifiable indication the employee understood the performance expectations through the progressive corrective action process.
   - There is some form of verification that the employee understood the consequences of not meeting those expectations.

2. **Schedule the termination meeting.**
   Make sure that:

   - The exiting employee has time to begin the adjustment before the end of the workday and before the weekend.
   - You can personally notify remaining employees and monitor their reactions.
   - You can notify their departments, if appropriate.

3. **Prepare your script.**
   Many managers find it helpful to write out what they plan to say and to go over their script several times. They don't read it word-for-word during the actual termination, but the preparation readies them for just about any kind of scenario. They plan what they might say if the person argues or becomes angry. Anticipate the employee's responsible reactions and think through how best to respond.

Handling Difficult Situations

1. **The employee doesn't say anything.**
   Some employees become emotional after hearing of their termination and respond by crying, Have some tissues on hand and within easy reach.

   The best way to respond is to sit back for a few moments and let the person cry even though this may be uncomfortable. Most people regain their composure just after a few minutes. When you see this start to happen you can say something like:

   > "I know this isn't an easy time for you. But when you're ready, let's move on with our meeting and let me go over some other points..."

   If the employee is ready, move ahead with the meeting. If the employee continues to cry, you may need to be more assertive to regain control. Remember, however, you must continue to show that the company cares.

   Sometimes repeating your message about continuing the meeting is enough to bring the employee around. Sometimes the message needs to be repeated several times, firmly, but with a caring tone.

Once in a great while, you may find it necessary to ask if the person needs a few minutes to be alone. In that case, the manager, and the witness excuse themselves from the room. You may want to monitor the office for the safety and well-being of the employee and others. When you return, you may say something like:

> "We know this is not an easy situation, but we believe it will be the most helpful if we can continue with the meeting. There is some important information we need to briefly review with you and then you can have time to yourself. Let me tell you what the company will be doing to help you through this transition..."

Do not assume that only women cry when told of job termination. Sometimes the employee who cries is the one you least expect to respond in that way.

2. **The employee gets angry.**
   Unfortunately, people seem to be less in control of their anger today than they were in the past. You may encounter some anger that is directed not only at the company but also to you as the messenger.

   Do not get pulled into the same kind of behavior and return with anger. If the employee's anger begins to move from verbal to physical, you obviously need to take preventive action. That is another reason always to have at least two people present during a termination meeting. The exiting employee is less likely to become aggressively hostile if s/he must confront two representatives of the company.

   Allow the employee to vent his or her anger – but maintain control. When the employee has calmed down say something like:

"Roy, your anger may be a normal reaction but it won't change things. The company does care about you and we will be providing some assistance during this transition. I'd like to continue with our meeting so we can go over what some of this assistance includes..."

Don't argue. If you begin to argue, you might say things that should not be said and you will only serve to fuel the employee's anger.

Don't respond in anger. When you respond in anger, you not only have lost control of the situation, but you demonstrate to the employee that you and the company really don't care about people.

Stay in control. Take a few breaths. Keep your voice calm. Don't raise your pitch.

3. **The employee wants to see the boss.**
   Sometimes an employee may insist upon seeing your boss or even the CEO.

Agree to plan for the terminated employee to see your boss or an upper-level executive. Let the employee know that these senior-level people are aware of the termination decision, have approved it and will not reverse it.

"Roy, I'm sure that Bob will see you after we're through with our meeting. But we do have to finish our meeting first. You should know that Bob is aware of your termination and has given approval. The decision will not be changed. But if you still want to see him when we're through, we can call his office to set up an appointment."

4. **The employee refuses to leave the building.**
   The best solution is not to allow this situation to arise by walking the employee from the building immediately following the termination. Occasionally, even after the employee has agreed to leave, the exiting employee won't exit – the longer they stay, the greater the disruption. When this occurs, be considerate yet firm and approach the exiting employee directly.

   "Sandy, I really need to ask for your cooperation. Your staying and talking with others is causing a lot of disruption and some people are feeling uncomfortable. We agreed that you were leaving right away. I'm going to ask you to make good on your agreement to the leave the offices as agreed."

   If the employee still does not leave, call security, and ask for assistance in walking the employee off the premises. This is obviously not a desirable scenario, but sometimes it is better than allowing the employee to remain and create trouble.

5. **The employee becomes physical.**
   If you suspect that the soon-terminated employee may become physically aggressive, seek specialized assistance from a local security agency or your local police department.

   - Be certain that the room in which you will be meeting has been primed by removing any articles and objects that could easily be picked up and thrown.
   - Have security alerted, informed of the situation, and prepared to help.
   - Be certain that you and another company representative conduct the termination meeting. As mentioned earlier, an employee will find it more difficult to become hostile and aggressive.

The percentage of termination discussions that result in physical violence is small. If you plan carefully and have considered all aspects of the termination meeting, you probably will never have to deal with a physical reaction from a terminated employee.

6. **The employee has committed gross misconduct.**
   Instances of gross misconduct call for special policies and procedures. Gross misconduct should be defined in the company's handbook and typically included: fighting, willful negligence, stealing and using drugs on the job. The following procedures are recommended for instances of gross misconduct:

   a. **Isolate the employee as soon as a gross misconduct has been identified.**
      Escort the employee to a conference room or the manager's office where the employee will not have contact with other employees. You do not want the employee to have access to others and build sympathy or distort events.

   b. **Involve other decision makers.**
      With the employee isolated, the supervisor and appropriate managers can calmly review the situation, call Human Resources, and decide. Even if they decide to terminate the employee at that moment, they must still complete the appropriate paperwork prior to giving the termination notice.

   c. **Document the decision.**
      Even before the termination notice is given to the employee, the manager should prepare a written summary of the incident and their decision to terminate.

   d. **Terminate and escort (only when necessary).**
      Inform the employee of the termination and that it is effective immediately. A manager can help or witness

gathering of personal articles from the employee's workstation and then the employee should be walked off the premises.

Dealing With The Remaining Staff

Many organizations treat resignations and/or terminations with a wall of silence. It appears at times to be an attempt to rewrite history. The empty desk or chair is treated like it was never occupied in the first place. This may reflect the manager's discomfort with the separation process or it can be a lack of knowledge or confidence in dealing with the situation professionally. Ignoring or trivializing the incident does not change the reality.

The remaining employees have questions, perceptions, and perhaps, fears that must be addressed.

It is important to meet with the remaining work group (those most affected by the separation) and address the issue in a straightforward manner.

- Acknowledge that the separated employee is no longer with the organization.
- Maintain the confidentiality of the circumstances relating to the separated employee.
- Acknowledge the workload requirements of the staff. Who will handle the responsibilities? Will the position be filled?

The predictable responses of the rest of the staff will be that approximately 10% of them are angry. They perceive you were unfair and mistreated their friend. Approximately 10% of them are happy. They disliked the terminated employee and perceived you were negligent in not dismissing him or her sooner. The other 80% of them accepted the facts and are ready to get on with their lives.

Effective use of the disciplinary process is an especially useful tool in turning around or eliminating poor performance and disruptive behavior. Understanding the process is not easy – it is complex and compounded by legal, moral, and policy issues that challenge any manager and every organization. Used properly, the disciplinary process is an asset. Used improperly, it is a nightmare, and when we fail to use it at all, it is chaos.

Conducting a Layoff Conversation

As economic conditions continue to be challenging for businesses the need to unexpectedly reduce staff also continues. There is a delicate balance between business needs and the need to ensure positive engagement of your employees in all matters. Should you ever need to prepare for this challenging business situation, these tips will help address business needs while creating an interaction that will engage your employees in a helpful, safe, and constructive way.

Pre-Meeting Preparation

- Understand that informing a person of a job loss is a difficult and stressful task; a successful outcome requires preparation and good instincts. Draw on any personal experience you have with this, what did you like about any interaction what did you dislike? Use those experiences for thoughtful preparation.
- Become thoroughly familiar with the Reduction in Staff process and the content of any separation materials. Gather information and prepare to discuss any benefit continuations, forms provided or placement assistance etc.).
- Plan to meet with the employee. Consider travel distances where applicable, location, date, time, and space needs. Open space offices or conference rooms where there is free flow of movement are best. Be cautious of office spaces where any one individual, may be boxed into the space without clear access to the door.
- Discuss with Human Resources or Executive Management any possible problems you feel could occur or any concerns

you may have about the notification, the employee or the documents being presented. Arrange for another manager to be with you during the meeting(s).

- Anticipate questions that you could be asked by the employee and find the answers. Potentially, one of an employee's most immediate needs or concerns during a notification meeting, is the concern for their financial security so make sure you are prepared to address this (explained later).

- Be aware that the release process can be emotional for all parties including you; prepare for this potential. Tissues and bottled water, while may seem melodramatic can serve to be of great comfort in calming emotions and provide a sense of compassion.

- Be prepared for "push back". An employee may want to debate the need for this reduction particularly in comparison to others.

- Practice and rehearse the message you will deliver. It is perfectly acceptable to use other managers to role play these situations in advance for an opportunity to rehearse what might be unexpected situations, questions, or reactions.

- Assess the impact of losing the employee on co-workers and customers. After reductions in staff there is a heightened sensitivity in those that remain, that may include questions like, who else may be affected, how long will reductions continue, who is going to do any work left by this new gap, etc.? Think of such things and prepare for that discussion. You can read more about that in Post Meeting.

The Notification Meeting

The primary purpose of the notification meeting is twofold: (1) to inform the employee that his/her job has been placed in lay-off or reduction in staff status and that their position is being eliminated causing their separation from employment which requires an immediate effective date and (2) to keep the person optimistic about the company and their future while preserving their dignity. These meetings can take anywhere from 30 minutes to over an hour depending on the individual employee, their questions, and individual reactions.

Your Role Is The Informer.

- The meeting should be private apart from one management witness and uninterrupted. Cell phones and landline phones should be silenced. Your employee needs to know that you have taken measures to ensure that they know your communications with them are your sole top priority.
- Don't procrastinate -get directly to the point; announce the action calmly; stick with the script (see below); control the flow of the meeting; keep the employee focused.
- Do not make any comments, even if well intended, that could compromise the decision to reduce the workforce. Stay away from discussions that could confuse the primary message, (i.e., the notification meeting is not about employee performance or personal issues). employees may want to discuss how busy they have been, excessive workloads that require them to remain on or outstanding assignments. Keep focused on relaying the message, thanking the employee for their selflessness and concern of the organization but the decision to move forward is irreversible.
- Be direct and firm as this will assure the person knows the decision is final. It is also important to be sensitive and compassionate to the person's situation. Use of facial expression and empathetic body language can help to soften the need to be direct. Don't use terms such as "unfortunately, unluckily, regrettably, sadly... These terms may create emotional negativity that the communication

does not need. Use words that are neutral such as necessary, required, essential.

- Don't blame others for the actions being taken or allow the employee to do so. Remind the employee that it is solely due to economic conditions, business downturns or similar business environment issues that have caused this workforce change.
- Don't become defensive, argumentative, or confrontational- --your role is not to justify the decision that has been made. Should employees comment about reasons other than that which you have already addressed, advise the employee that you appreciate their feedback but the reasons remain as stated.
- Listen. It is important to ensure you closely listen and document anything that could lead to a potential problem later. Comments such as an employee's intent to let everyone at work know, use social media negatively, intent to notify an attorney or similar comments should be noted. Advising the employee that, while it has been a mutually difficult communication, you were optimistic that the positive experiences with the organization thus far wouldn't be completely jeopardized due to this necessary business decision. Thereafter notify your Executive management or Human Resources immediately.
- Review and complete any required forms with the employee. It is advised that you provide them with a memo or letter for all parties' signature outlining the conversation contents. A brief one-page document is sufficient to assist with any explanations they need to make to future prospective employers or for unemployment purposes should documentation be required.
- Collect or plan to collect ALL company property and tie up any business processes. Inform the employee that access to voice mail, email, computer systems will be discontinued and any expense items outstanding (if applicable) should be turned in by the end of the business day. It is helpful to

have a checklist of items to ensure nothing is overlooked. Items such as office keys, computer equipment, company issued cell phones and parking cards are likely to be included. Employees with desks or offices will require time to collect any personal effects. It is recommended that they return to their offices/desks to do so or the employee can return during off hours ensuring you are available to supervise the exit. (Contact HBL Resources if you are interested in our comprehensive Separation Packet).

- Offer support and encouragement. The employee should be given any information regarding outplacement assistance offered by the company. In the event no formal outplacement assistance is contracted, at a minimum the employer should provide a current list of similar open positions in the local market, a list of web-based job boards in the respective industry, information, and process regarding filing an unemployment claim and like information. This helps the employee become immediately focused on completing these processes during the transition between employers. Exit the employee in a dignified manner. Unless there is a serious fear of theft of key business property, verbal retaliation, violence in the workplace or the like, it is not advisable to oversee the employee's desk/office cleanup or to "escort" the employee off premises. The individual who witnessed the discussion could accompany the employee after the conversation and indicate they are there to assist with transportation of personal affects. In this way the employer is knowledgeable of the employee's whereabouts without the perception of an obvious escort.

- If you feel there is a need to secure the environment due to the employee's potential for violence or other negative behavior you may want to schedule the meeting for non-peak hours or non-peak days. Additionally, you should contact your human resources department, security designate or another third party to assist in preparedness.

- The employee may become resistant, defensive and/or non-accepting of the action, may want to plead a case or bargain for another opportunity: Stay in control of the meeting and your emotions at all times. If the employee sees you flustered or out of control that is likely going to be their mirrored emotion. Keep a calm, yet firm tone which can help to de-escalate an elevating tone or voice of an employee.

- The person may want to speak with a "decision maker": Hopefully, your organization has an engaging enough environment that a feeling of open communication exists. In the event the "decision maker" is agreeable to receiving communication, advise the employee that you will notify the "decision maker" of their interest in speaking with them. Obtain the best number, day(s), and time(s) from the employee for the "decision maker" to contact them, then ensure they do so. The communication should be no different than that which was stated in the Notification Meeting. Be certain to advise the decision maker of any relevant comments made by the employee during the notification meeting. In the event the decision maker is not made available for continued communications, inform the employee of that decision and that you would directly relay any information they wanted. Then, be certain to do so.

- The employee may ask the "why me?" questions or any number of others. It is important to anticipate what may be asked and be prepared with a brief answer. Review *The Questions* below for assistance on commonly asked questions.

- The person may threaten a lawsuit or other retaliation: Let the person know that he/she is free to make whatever contacts they feel appropriate and that, while it has been a mutually difficult communication, you were optimistic that the positive experiences with the organization thus far wouldn't be completely jeopardized due to this necessary business decision.

- The employee may try to make the issue personal or about performance, may argue about a person being retained who they believe is less capable, has less tenure, etc.: Reiterate that the decision is not about performance or about other employees. Be certain to get the discussion focused back on the main topic. Keep the focus of the reduction focused on the position held and not on the individual employee.

Questions That may be Asked

"Why Do You Want to Meet?" When you inform the employee that you need to meet with him or her, you may be asked "why?" Don't lie. Awkward as it may feel, it is best to merely state that you will discuss the reason when you meet. If you feel compelled to tell the person what action is to take place, consult with your Human Resources Department or Executive Management beforehand to discuss the situation.

"Why Me?" The "why me?" question is a natural reactive question. Unfortunately, it has no answer that will satisfy the employee. The response should be only that "the decisions were difficult and (if it is the case), that many good people were affected." The employee may inquire about who is being retained, as they will often want to compare themselves and make a case for their retention. This too is not unusual, but you cannot comment on that.

Who made this decision? It is important to be as transparent as possible, if a group or committee made the decision then it is ok to indicate such or simply indicate an executive decision or management decision. If you are the only person responsible for the workforce (owner, president etc.) it is fair to indicate it is a decision you have had to make.

Who can I talk to regarding getting this decision changed? It is expected that if you are conducting a Reduction in Staff Notification meeting, all efforts have been made to avoid this Reduction in Staff and that all other solutions have been exhausted. Inform the employee that the decision was not made lightly *and* cannot be changed.

Are there any other jobs in the company? It is expected that if you are conducting a Reduction in Staff Notification meeting, all efforts have been made to avoid this Reduction in Staff and that all other solutions have been exhausted. Inform the employee that the decision was not made lightly and cannot be changed.

Can I keep my job if I take a pay cut? It is expected that if you are conducting a Reduction in Staff Notification meeting, all efforts have been made to avoid this Reduction In Staff and that all other solutions have been exhausted. Inform the employee that the decision was not made lightly and cannot be changed. It is ok to be honest and advise the employee that cuts in pay, reduced salaries or delayed raises, have previously been invoked to avoid this Reduction in Staff step.

Who else is being released? If there will be other employees affected, simply advise the employee that names of others must be kept confidential at this time and ask the employee to empathize with the need to keep these names confidential.

Post Meeting

- Notify the Human Resources Department or Executive Management that the employee has been advised/exited the premises. Discuss any critical issues because of the conversation or key information contained within your notes.
- When multiple Reductions are necessary it is advisable to hold an employee/departmental meeting/conference call. You should inform employees about the actions that have taken place, particularly the need to reduce the staff. Understand and recognize that your people have lost

friends and may have their own anxieties. It is ok to share the business environment which necessitated the decision. Get people re-focused quickly on the business.

- Be honest about what you know and can share; discuss workload and/or support concerns/needs; focus on the positives and the continued team approach.
- Do not assume "business as usual" acceptance. Be accessible to your people; keep an open door to listen to individual employee concerns and welcome their comments.
- Thank people for their continued support; restate the business objectives; make no promises or guarantees about the future (a good response is "the future is up to us"). It is reassuring and can often calm any fears to advise the employees remaining that while "the future is up to us" all necessary notification discussions have taken place for the business needs at this time.
- Make contact and meet with, any new person coming into your group that may have entered because of any workforce reductions or lateral moves. Introduce them to others and orient them to the business unit or departments "norms".
- You may consider advising the appropriate customers about internal changes that may affect them. Nothing is worse than for a customer than to call and be surprised that they have been assigned a new company contact. Let them know before they need to make contact. Introduce them to new contacts and service providers as appropriate to ensure they have an immediate sense of comfort with their new representative.
- Of course, never make any disparaging remarks about anyone leaving the company doing so could put the business at risk.

INDEX

NEXT STEP
RESOURCES

READY TO CONTINUE
Transforming The Human in Human Resources®

Connect With Like Minded Individuals in our Communities!

Explore our Membership Options
https://thecompletemanagermakeover.com/memberships-for-managers
https://thecompletemanagermakeover.com/memberships-for-business-owners

Explore our Community
https://thecompletemanagermakeover.com/our-community

Listen to Our Podcasts
https://thecompletemanagermakeover.com/our-podcasts/

DOWNLOAD
the Complete Curriculum & Memberships Brochure

**Hire Lisa to Speak at your Event
or Facilitate Training for your Organization**

Find out more at LisaIPerez.com

Connect with Lisa

JOIN THE MOVEMENT

National Management Training Week
www.NationalDayCalendar.com

GET INVOLVED IN NATIONAL
MANAGEMENT TRAINING WEEK
RECEIVE YOUR OFFICIAL TOOLKIT
TO BEGIN PREPRATIONS TODAY!

Get The Complete Manager Makeover FULL COLOR Bookmarks Reference Set to keep The CMM tips and techniques at your fingertips!

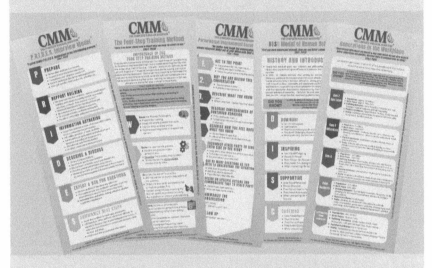

Available ONLY for a LIMITED TIME!
Full Color Set ONLY $19.97